UNLOCKING THE BIBLE

OLD TESTAMENT BOOK III

Poems of Worship and Wisdom

UNLOCKING THE BIBLE

OLD TESTAMENT BOOK III

Poems of Worship and Wisdom

David Pawson

with Andy Peck

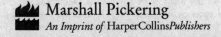

Marshall Pickering
An Imprint of HarperCollins*Publishers*

Marshall Pickering is an Imprint of
HarperCollins*Religious*
Part of HarperCollins*Publishers*
77–85 Fulham Palace Road, London W6 8JB

First published in Great Britain in 2000
by Marshall Pickering

1 3 5 7 9 10 8 6 4 2

A catalogue record for this book is
available from the British Library

ISBN 0 551 03189 1

Printed and bound in Great Britain by
Caledonian International Book Manufacturing Ltd, Glasgow

CONTENTS

INTRODUCTION

OLD TESTAMENT BOOK III

I suppose this all started in Arabia, in 1957. I was then a chaplain in the Royal Air Force, looking after the spiritual welfare of all those who were not C.E. (Church of England) or R.C. (Roman Catholic) but O.D. (other denominations – Methodist to Salvationist, Buddhist to atheist). I was responsible for a string of stations from the Red Sea to the Persian Gulf. In most there was not even a congregation to call a 'church', never mind a building.

In civilian life I had been a Methodist minister working anywhere from the Shetland Islands to the Thames Valley. In that denomination it was only necessary to prepare a few sermons each quarter, which were hawked around a 'circuit' of chapels. Mine had mostly been of the 'text' type (talking about a single verse) or the 'topic' type (talking about a single subject with many verses from all over the Bible). In both I was as guilty as any of taking texts out of context before I realized that chapter and verse numbers were neither inspired nor intended by God and had done immense damage to Scripture, not least by changing the meaning of 'text' from a whole book to a single sentence. The Bible had become a compendium of 'proof-texts', picked out at will and used to support almost anything a preacher wanted to say.

With a pocketful of sermons based on this questionable technique, I found myself in uniform, facing very different congregations – all male instead of the lifeboat-style gatherings I had been used to: women and children first. My meagre stock of messages soon ran out. Some of them had gone down like a lead balloon, especially in compulsory parade services in England before I was posted overseas.

So here I was in Aden, virtually starting a church from scratch, from the Permanent Staff and temporary National Servicemen of Her Majesty's youngest armed service. How could I get these men interested in the Christian faith and then committed to it?

Something (I would now say: Someone) prompted me to announce that I would give a series of talks over a few months, which would take us right through the Bible ('from Generation to Revolution'!).

It was to prove a voyage of discovery for all of us. The Bible became a new book when seen as a whole. To use a well-worn cliché, we had failed to see the wood for the trees. Now God's plan and purpose were unfolding in a fresh way. The men were getting something big enough to sink their teeth into. The thought of being part of a cosmic rescue was a powerful motivation. The Bible story was seen as both real and relevant.

Of course, my 'overview' was at that time quite simple, even naive. I felt like that American tourist who 'did' the British Museum in 20 minutes – and could have done it in 10 if he'd had his running shoes! We raced through the centuries, giving some books of the Bible little more than a passing glance.

But the results surpassed my expectations and set the course for the rest of my life and ministry. I had become a 'Bible teacher', albeit in embryo. My ambition to share the excitement of knowing the whole Bible became a passion.

When I returned to 'normal' church life, I resolved to take my congregation through the whole Bible in a decade (if they put up with me that long). This involved tackling about one 'chapter' at every service. This took a lot of time, both in preparation (an hour in the study for every 10 minutes in the pulpit) and delivery (45–50 minutes). The ratio was similar to that of cooking and eating a meal.

The effect of this systematic 'exposition' of Scripture confirmed its rightness. A real hunger for God's Word was revealed. People began to *come* from far and wide, 'to recharge their batteries' as some explained. Soon this traffic was reversed. Tape recordings, first prepared for the sick and housebound, now began to *go* far and wide, ultimately in hundreds of thousands to 120 countries. No one was more surprised than I.

Leaving Gold Hill in Buckinghamshire for Guildford in Surrey, I found myself sharing in the design and building of the Millmead Centre, which contained an ideal auditorium for continuing this teaching ministry. When it was opened, we decided to associate it with the whole Bible by reading it aloud right through without stopping. It took us 84 hours, from Sunday evening until Thursday morning, each person reading for 15 minutes before passing the Bible on to someone else. We used the 'Living' version, the easiest both to read and to listen to, with the heart as well as the mind.

We did not know what to expect, but the event seemed to capture the public imagination. Even the mayor wanted to take part and by sheer coincidence (or providence) found himself reading about a husband who was 'well known, for he sits in the council chamber with the other civic leaders' (Proverbs 31:23). He insisted on taking a copy home for his wife. Another lady dropped in on her way to see her solicitor about the legal termination of her marriage and found herself reading, 'I hate divorce, says the Lord'. She never went to the lawyer.

An aggregate of 2,000 people attended and bought half a ton of Bibles. Some came for half an hour and were still there hours later, muttering to themselves, 'Well, maybe just one more book and then I really must go.'

It was the first time many, including our most regular attenders, had ever heard a book of the Bible read straight through. In most churches only a few sentences are read each week and then not always consecutively. What other book would get anyone interested, much less excited, if treated in this way?

So on Sundays we worked through the whole Bible book by book. For the Bible is not one book, but many – in fact, it is a whole library (the word *biblia* in Latin and Greek is plural: 'books'). And not just many books, but many *kinds* of books – history, law, letters, songs, etc. It became necessary, when we had finished studying one book, and were starting on another, to begin with a special introduction covering very basic questions: What kind of book is this? When was it written? Who wrote it? Who was it written for? Above all, *why* was it written? The answer to that last question provided the 'key' to unlock its message. Nothing in that book could be fully understood unless seen as part of the whole. The context of every 'text' was not just the paragraph or the section but fundamentally the whole book itself.

By now, I was becoming more widely known as a Bible teacher and was invited to colleges, conferences and conventions – at first in this country, but increasingly overseas, where tapes had opened doors and prepared the way. I enjoy meeting new people and seeing new places, but the novelty of sitting in a jumbo jet wears off in 10 minutes!

Everywhere I went I found the same eager desire to know God's Word. I praised God for the invention of recording cassettes which, unlike video systems, are standardized the world over. They were helping to plug a real hole in so many places. There is so much successful evangelism but so little teaching ministry to stabilize, develop and mature converts.

I might have continued along these lines until the end of my active ministry, but the Lord had another surprise for me, which was the last link in the chain that led to the publication of these volumes.

In the early 1990s, Bernard Thompson, a friend pastoring a church in Wallingford, near Oxford, asked me to speak at a short series of united meetings with the aim of increasing interest in and knowledge of the Bible – an objective guaranteed to hook me!

I said I would come once a month and speak for three hours about one book in the Bible (with a coffee break in the middle!). In return, I asked those attending to read that book right through before and after my visit. During the following weeks preachers were to base their sermons and house group discussions on the same book. All this would hopefully mean familiarity at least with that one book.

My purpose was two-fold. On the one hand, to get people so interested in that book that they could hardly wait to read it. On the other hand, to give them enough insight and information so that when they did read it they would be excited by their ability to understand it. To help with both, I used pictures, charts, maps and models.

This approach really caught on. After just four months I was pressed to book dates for the next five years, to cover all 66 books! I laughingly declined, saying I might be in heaven long before then (in fact, I have rarely booked anything more than six months ahead, not wanting to mortgage the future, or presume that I have one). But the Lord had other plans and enabled me to complete the marathon.

Anchor Recordings (72, The Street, Kennington, Ashford, Kent TN24 9HS) have distributed my tapes for the last 20 years and when the Director, Jim Harris, heard the recordings of these meetings, he urged me to consider putting them on video. He arranged for cameras and crew to come to High Leigh Conference Centre, its main hall 'converted' into a studio, for three days at a time, enabling 18 programmes to be made with an invited audience. It took another five years to complete this project, which was distributed under the title 'Unlocking the Bible'.

Now these videos are travelling around the world. They are being used in house groups, churches, colleges, the armed forces, gypsy camps, prisons and on cable television networks. During an extended visit to Malaysia, they were being snapped up at a rate of a thousand a week. They have infiltrated all six continents, including Antarctica!

More than one have called this my 'legacy to the church'. Certainly it is the fruit of many years' work. And I am now in my seventieth year on planet earth, though I do not think the Lord has finished with me yet. But I did think this particular task had reached its conclusion. I was mistaken.

HarperCollins approached me with a view to publishing this material in a series of volumes. For the last decade or so I had been writing books for other publishers, so was already convinced that this was a good means of spreading God's Word. Nevertheless, I had two huge reservations about this proposal which made me very hesitant. One was due to the way the material had been prepared and the other related to the way it had been delivered. I shall explain them in reverse order.

First, I have never written out in full any sermon, lecture or talk. I speak from notes, sometimes pages of them. I have been concerned about communication as much as content and intuitively knew that a full manuscript interrupts the rapport between speaker and audience, not least by diverting his eyes from the listeners. Speech that is more spontaneous can respond to reactions as well as express more emotions.

The result is that my speaking and writing styles are very different, each adapted to its own function. I enjoy listening to my tapes and can be deeply moved by myself. I am enthusiastic about reading one of my new publications, often telling my wife, 'This really *is* good stuff!' But when I read a transcript of what I have said, I am ashamed and even appalled. Such repetition of words and phrases! Such rambling, even incomplete sentences! Such a mixture of verb tenses, particularly past and present! Do I really abuse the Queen's English like this? The evidence is irrefutable.

I made it clear that I could not possibly contemplate writing out all this material in full. It has taken most of one lifetime anyway and I do not have another. True, transcripts of the talks had already been made, with a view to translating and dubbing the videos into other languages such as Spanish and Chinese. But the thought of these being printed as they were horrified me. Perhaps this is a final struggle with pride, but the contrast with my written books, over which I took such time and trouble, was more than I could bear.

I was assured that copy editors correct most grammatical blunders. But the main remedy proposed was to employ a 'ghostwriter' who was in tune with me and my ministry, to adapt the material for printing. An introduction to the person chosen, Andy Peck, gave me every confidence that he could do the job, even though the result would not be what I would have written – nor, for that matter, what he would have written himself.

I gave him all the notes, tapes, videos and transcripts, but these volumes are as much his work as mine. He has worked incredibly hard and I am deeply grateful to him for enabling me to reach many more with the truth that sets people free. If one gets a prophet's reward for merely giving the prophet a drink of water, I can only thank the Lord for the reward Andy will get for this immense labour of love.

Second, I have never kept careful records of my sources. This is partly because the Lord blessed me with a reasonably good memory for such things as quotations and illustrations and perhaps also because I have never used secretarial assistance.

Books have played a major role in my work – three tons of them, according to the last furniture remover we employed, filling two rooms and a garden shed. They are in three categories: those I have read, those I intend to read and those I will never read! They have been such a blessing to me and such a bane to my wife.

The largest section by far is filled with Bible commentaries. When preparing a Bible study, I have looked up all relevant writers, but only after I have prepared as much as I can on my own. Then I have both added to and corrected my efforts in the light of scholarly and devotional writings.

It would be impossible to name all those to whom I have been indebted. Like many others I devoured William Barclays' *Daily Bible Readings* as soon as they were issued back in the 1950s. His knowledge of New Testament background and vocabulary was invaluable and his simple and clear style a model to follow, though I later came to question his 'liberal' interpretations. John Stott, Merill Tenney, Gordon Fee and William Hendrickson were among those who opened up the New Testament for me, while Alec Motyer, G. T. Wenham and Derek Kidner did the same for the Old. And time would fail to tell of Denney, Lightfoot, Nygren, Robinson, Adam Smith, Howard, Ellison, Mullen, Ladd, Atkinson, Green, Beasley-Murray, Snaith, Marshall, Morris, Pink and many many others. Nor must I forget two remarkable little books from the pens of women: *What the Bible is all about* by Henrietta Mears and *Christ in all the Scriptures* by A. M. Hodgkin. To have sat at their feet has been an inestimable privilege. I have always regarded a willingness to learn as one of the fundamental qualifications to be a teacher.

I soaked up all these sources like a sponge. I remembered so much of *what* I read, but could not easily recall *where* I had read it. This did not seem to matter too much when gathering material for preaching, since most of these writers were precisely aiming to help preachers and did not expect to be constantly quoted. Indeed, a sermon full of attributed quotations can be distracting, if not misinterpreted as name-dropping or indirectly claiming to be well read. As could my previous paragraph!

But printing, unlike preaching, is subject to copyright, since royalties are involved. And the fear of breaching this held me back from allowing any of my spoken ministry to be reproduced in print. It would be out of the question to trace back 40 years' scrounging and even if that were possible, the necessary footnotes and acknowledgements could double the size and price of these volumes.

The alternative was to deny access to my material for those who could most benefit from it, which my publisher persuaded me would be wrong. At least I was responsible for collecting and collating it all, but I dare to believe that there is sufficient original contribution to justify its release.

I can only offer an apology and my gratitude to all those whose studies I have plundered over the years, whether in small or large amounts, hoping they might see this as an example of that imitation which is the sincerest form of flattery. To use another quotation I read somewhere: 'Certain authors, speaking of their works, say "my book" … They would do better to say "our book" … because there is in them usually more of other people's than their own' (the original came from Pascal).

So here is 'our' book! I suppose I am what the French bluntly call a 'vulgarizer'. That is someone who takes what the academics teach and makes it simple enough for the 'common' people to understand. I am content with that. As one old lady said to me, after I had expounded a quite profound passage of Scripture, 'You broke it up small enough for us to take it in.' I have, in fact, always aimed so to teach that a 12-year-old boy could understand and remember my message.

Some readers will be disappointed, even frustrated, with the paucity of text references, especially if they want to check me out! But their absence is intentional. God gave us his Word in books, but not in chapters and verses. That was the work of two bishops, French and Irish, centuries later. It became easier to find a 'text' and to ignore context. How many Christians who quote John 3:16 can recite verses 15 and 17? Many no longer 'search the scriptures'; they simply look them up (given the numbers). So I have followed the apostles' habit of naming the authors only – 'as Isaiah or David or Samuel said'. For example, the Bible says that God whistles. Where on earth does it say that? In the book of Isaiah. Whereabouts? Go and find out for yourself. Then you'll also find out when he did and why he did. And you'll have the satisfaction of having discovered all that by yourself.

One final word. Behind my hope that these introductions to the Bible books will help you to get to know and love them more than you did lies a much greater and deeper longing – that you will also come to know better and love more the subject of all the books, the Lord Himself. I was deeply touched by the remark of someone who had watched all the videos within a matter of days: 'I know so much more about the Bible now, but the biggest thing was that I felt the heart of God as never before.'

What more could a Bible teacher ask? May you experience the same as you read these pages and join me in saying: Praise Father, Son and Holy Spirit.

J. David Pawson
Sherborne St John, 1999

Yes, I thought I knew my Bible,
Reading piecemeal, hit or miss:
Now a part of John or Matthew,
Then a bit of Genesis.

Certain chapters of Isaiah,
Certain psalms, the twenty-third,
First of Proverbs, twelfth of Romans –
Yes, I thought I knew the Word.

But I found that thorough reading
Was a different thing to do
And the way was unfamiliar
When I read my Bible through.

You who like to play at Bible,
Dip and dabble here and there,
Just before you kneel all weary,
Yawning through a hurried prayer.

You who treat this crown of writings
As you treat no other book:
Just a paragraph disjointed,
Just a crude impatient look.

Try a worthier procedure,
Try a broad and steady view;
You will kneel in awesome wonder
When you read the Bible through.

Author unknown

INTRODUCTION TO HEBREW POETRY

Poetry is one of a number of forms of literature that are used in the Old Testament. It is found in the prophets and in the 'writings' or 'wisdom literature', notably in the Psalms, the Book of Job and the Song of Songs. But since Hebrew poetry is so different from English poetry, we need to consider it in some detail if we are to receive the full benefit from these parts of God's Word.

It is relatively easy to spot poetry in modern Bibles, since the print is arranged differently from prose sections. Prose has long sentences and full columns, poetry short sentences with larger spaces to set it apart. A cursory glance at a Bible shows that there is substantially more poetry in the Old Testament than in the New.

Prose is the more natural and spontaneous way to communicate. People speak and write in prose using a variety of sentence lengths to communicate their point. Poetry is an abnormal and artificial way of writing. It needs to be prepared beforehand, it requires considerable thought and the words used need to obey the rules of poetic style. We might ask why it is that poetry is used when prose is so much easier.

For example, imagine me coming home and saying to Enid, my wife,

I'm ready for my supper, wife.
Oh good, it's pies and peas.
You've given me a dirty knife –
I'd like a clean one, please!
And since there is no second course,
I'll have some more tomato sauce!

If I talked like that it would mean that I had thought about my words beforehand. But the artificiality of talking in poetry in such a setting would hamper clear communication!

A deeper effect

Why bother to compose poetry?

Poetry has a much deeper effect on people than prose. Poetry can penetrate parts of the personality that prose would leave untouched.

Deeper into the mind

Poetry is more easily remembered than prose, especially when set to music. It touches the intuitive and artistic part of the brain, that can be left unmoved by the ordered arguments of prose.

So poems from our school days may be remembered decades later, while lectures are forgotten by the next week. For this reason we generally learn our theology from hymns and choruses, which is why it's important to make sure that the songs used in worship have Bible-based content.

Deeper into the heart

Poetry is used in greeting cards because it is a more effective way of moving the heart of the recipient. It can evoke warm emotions, while the same sentiments expressed in prose would leave the reader unmoved.

Consider the following poem:

> They walked down the lane together,
> The sky was full of stars.
> Together they reached the farmyard gate,
> He lifted for her the bars.
> She neither smiled nor thanked him,
> Indeed, she knew not how,
> For he was just a farmer's boy,
> And she was a Jersey cow!

Whenever I have quoted this in a talk, the congregation has laughed. They expect romance but receive something ridiculous, which touches their sense of humour. If the same content were to be expressed in prose, I doubt if it would even raise a smile.

Deeper into the will

Poetry also affects our volitional powers. It moves us to the point where we are determined to act in a certain way. In schools poems have been used to instil values into pupils. War songs have been used throughout history to galvanize soldiers for action.

Consider this poem, entitled 'Indifference', by Studdert Kennedy, an army chaplain in World War I:

> When Jesus came to Golgotha, they hanged him on a tree,
> They drove great nails through hands and feet
>   and made a Calvary;
> They crowned him with a crown of thorns,
>   red were his wounds and deep,

> For those were crude and cruel days,
>   and human flesh was cheap.
>
> When Jesus came to Birmingham,
>   they simply passed him by,
> They never hurt a hair of him, they only let him die.
> For men had grown more tender
>   and they would not give him pain,
> They only passed him down the street
>   and left him in the rain.
>
> Still Jesus cried 'Forgive them,
>   for they know not what they do'
> And still it rained the wintry rain
>   that drenched him through and through.
> The crowds went home and left the streets
>   without a soul to see,
> That Jesus crouched against a wall, and cried for Calvary.

There is something about the rhythm and the careful choice of words in that poem which compels us to examine our lives.

Beauty

Poetry touches the heart, the mind and the will by making words *beautiful* as well as meaningful. We are drawn to poems because the words are arranged in such a way that they appeal to our sense of beauty, balance, symmetry and proportion.

Just as a beautiful person has well-balanced features, so it is this balance that appeals to us in poetry.

There are three basic features of poetry that make the words beautiful for us: *rhyme*, *rhythm* and *repetition*.

Rhyme

Rhyme is a common feature of English poetry, but it is not generally found in Hebrew poetry. This classic nursery rhyme demonstrates a balance of rhyming words well:

> Jack and Jill went up the hill,
> To fetch a pail of water.
> Jack fell down and broke his crown
> And Jill came tumbling after.

It has a simple rhyme structure that is common to most nursery rhymes, and children have no trouble learning them.

Rhythm

The second feature of poetry that makes words beautiful is rhythm or metre, where the beat based on the syllables must fall on the correct words. For example:

> The boy stood on the burning deck
> Whence all but he had fled.
>
> *Mrs Hemans*

The poem has a 4/3 rhythm, a favourite for both Hebrew and English poetry, and often used in the metrical Psalms in Scotland. Take another example:

> The *Lord's* my *shep*herd, *I'll* not *want* – (4)
> He *makes* me *down* to *lie* (3)
> in *pas*tures *green* he *lead*eth *me* – (4)
> the *quiet wa*ters *by* – (3).
>
> *Francis Rous*

Good rhythm is dependent on the emphasis falling on the right syllable. When a hymn or chorus fails in this regard the effect is unpleasant. Take, for example, these two lines from a hymn:

> For *all* the *good* our *Father* does,
> God *and* king *of* us *all*.

The beat is placed on the wrong syllables and so emphasizes the wrong words. The hymn's beauty is lost.

Rhythm can also be used to shock the reader:

> Thirty days hath September,
> April, June and November;
> All the rest have thirty-one,
> Is that fair?!

The last line is startling because it breaks the rhythm and brings you up with a jolt.

Repetition

The third aspect of poetry that makes words beautiful is repetition. The repetition of a word or a line makes it poetic. There is a famous speech in Shakespeare's play *Julius Caesar* that repeats the line, 'And Brutus is an honourable man.' Or take this famous nursery rhyme that uses repetition:

> 'Baa, baa, black sheep, have you any wool?'
> 'Yes sir, yes sir, three bags full.'

The repetition may be of lines, phrases or even letters. Maybe you noticed how Studdert Kennedy uses words beginning with 'c' in his poem 'Indifference': 'crude', 'cruel', 'crouched' and 'cried'. They serve to emphasize the two 'c's that are the key to its theme: *cross* and *crucify*.

In other cases a refrain is used to emphasize a point. For example, Psalm 136 repeats the phrase, 'His love endures for ever.'

Other poems employ alliteration. In 'The Siege of Belgrade,' the first line of each verse is a consecutive letter of the alphabet, but this same letter is used for the main words in each verse. Psalm 119 is similar.

Wonder

Because poetry is partly about communicating pleasant sounds, the effect of poetry is often lost or diminished if it is just read silently. Poems are meant to be read aloud. There is something very satisfying about the sound of poetry. It brings a sense of wonder that isn't generally found in prose. It is no surprise, therefore, that poems are used in the worship of God. The Psalms (the Jews' hymn-book), are all in poetry. Prose is generally very difficult to sing, while poems lend themselves more readily to musical accompaniment.

Furthermore, poetry helps us to appreciate and express the sense of wonder that we feel as we worship. I will show what I mean by using a well-known poem:

> Twinkle, twinkle little star,
> How I wonder what you are.
> Up above the world so high,
> Like a diamond in the sky.
> *Jane Taylor*

It's possible to kill the child-like wonder in this poem by reducing it to scientific terms:

> Twinkle, twinkle little star,
> I don't wonder what you are.
> You're the cooling down of gasses,
> Forming into solid masses.

Let's take it a step further:

> Scintillate, scintillate, globule prolific,
> Fain would I fathom thy nature specific.
> Loftily poised in ether capacious,
> Closely resembling a gem carbonaceous.

Note the contrast between the language of science and that of poetry. The former is exact and cold, while the latter is less precise but evokes wonder and awe. This is what makes poetry such a good medium for worship. Hymns, songs, psalms and choruses help us to express something of the wonder and glory of God in a way that scientific forms of expression cannot.

Poetry is visual as well as verbal. It paints pictures in the mind. Imagination is very necessary to writing poetry. It uses metaphors, similes and images. For example, 'Twinkle, twinkle little star … like a diamond in the sky' helps to conjure a picture of a shining star.

Let's take Psalm 42 as another example:

> As the deer pants for streams of water,
> so my soul longs for God.

We imagine an animal panting, with its tongue hanging out, and that makes us think of our own thirst for God.

Sound and sense

English poetry is based on Greek and Roman poetry, where the emphasis is on the sound. Although there are other forms and styles, English poetry generally rhymes, while in Hebrew poetry, the emphasis is on the sense.

This distinction is especially clear in the English tradition of 'nonsense verse', of which Edward Lear and Lewis Carroll were the masters. Carroll's 'The Jabberwocky' is a prime example of this sort of poetry:

> 'Twas brillig, and the slithy toves
> Did gyre and gimble in the wabe;
> All mimsy were the borogroves,
> And the mome raths outgrabe.

Reading such poetry is a little like enjoying Pavarotti singing Italian opera without knowing the language, or enjoying pop music when the words are inaudible or meaningless. We haven't a clue what it is about but we like it anyway.

Such poems may 'move' us but they don't take us anywhere. Reading them may help us to relax and to appreciate life, but they don't affect the way we live.

Hebrew poetry is very different from the English style. Even in the original language, the emphasis is upon the sense of the words rather than the sound of them, which is one reason why there is very little rhyme in Hebrew poetry.

Parallelism

While rhythm is not unknown (especially the 4/3 and the 3/3 rhythms), Hebrew poetry is mostly based on a form of repetition called *parallelism*. The word refers to the correspondence that occurs between the phrases of a poetic line. Parallelism is the basic 'building block' of Hebrew poetry. It is used for:

- *Emphasis.* If something is said twice, we know it is important.
- *Response.* A couplet enables 'antiphonal' singing, in which two choirs sing to each other. One choir sings the first sentence and the other choir echoes it.
- *Balance.* Just as there is balance in a human body – two hands, two eyes, two ears, two arms, two legs – so the couplet helps us to understand the beauty of a thought.

Usually the repetition is in the form of couplets but the Psalms also contain some triplets and just a few quadruplets. Here is an example of a couplet, from Psalm 6:

> O Lord, do not rebuke me in your anger
> or discipline me in your wrath.

To 'rebuke' is to tell someone they are in the wrong, while to 'discipline' is to punish, so the second line develops the first line's thought a little further. Or take the next verse in this psalm:

> Be merciful to me, O Lord, for I am faint;
> O Lord, heal me, for my bones are in agony.

In the first line the psalmist feels faint, but in the second line he is in agony and needs healing. So once again the second line has taken the first line a little further. But note that it is the *sense* that is repeated, not the sound.

I am concious of the fact that analysing poetry is like taking a flower to pieces and looking at its parts. Analysis destroys the beauty. Nevertheless, I want to help you to understand what's going on when you read biblical poetry – why it was written and how it was written.

There are three different forms of parallelism:

Synonymous

In synonymous parallelism the same thought is expressed twice in different words. Let's take Psalm 2 as an example:

> Why do the *nations conspire*
> and the *peoples plot* in vain?
> The *kings* of the earth take their stand
> and the *rulers* gather together
> against the *Lord*
> and against his *Anointed One.*
> 'Let us break their *chains*,' they say,
> 'and throw off their *fetters*.'
> The One enthroned in heaven *laughs*;
> The Lord *scoffs* at them.
> Then he rebukes them in his *anger*
> and terrifies them in his *wrath*.

Note how the words in italic type in each couplet have the same meaning, but generally the second word is 'stronger' or 'heavier' than the first.

Antithetic

Antithetic parallelism functions like synonymous parallelism, but the second line contrasts with the first line. So, in this example from Psalm 126:

> Those who *sow* in tears
> will *reap* with songs of joy.

Two pairs are contrasted: 'sowing' and 'reaping', 'tears' and 'joy'. In the next verse we have the theme expanded:

> He who goes out *weeping*,
> carrying seed to *sow*,
> will return with songs of *joy*,
> carrying *sheaves* with him.

These two lines add more detail to the contrast. We now have going out with seed and returning with sheaves.

Synthetic

In synthetic parallelism the second phrase complements or supplements the first. It doesn't say the same thing or the opposite thing, but something that follows from the first phrase. For example:

> When the Lord brought back the captives to Zion,
> we were like men who dreamed.
>
> *from Psalm 126*

> The Lord is my shepherd, I shall not be in want.
>
> *from Psalm 23*

In these examples the second phrase is the result of the first. Psalm 23 is built on the synthetic pattern:

> He makes me lie down in green pastures,
> he leads me beside quiet waters.

The shepherd has to know where there are green pastures and quiet waters. But those two things together create a picture of a shepherd who really knows his job and cares for his sheep.

* * *

So we have three forms of Hebrew poetry but many varieties within these forms. Parallelism is not just in thought and word, but also in grammar. For example, in these lines from Psalm 2 the order of the words in the Hebrew is:

> Then he rebukes them in his anger
> and in his wrath he terrifies them.

The order of the verb, the object and the prepositional phrase is varied in the second line.

Tricolon

These three types of parallelism are often interrupted by irregularities. Sometimes the rhythm and pattern are broken. Sometimes, instead of two lines there are three lines together. This is called a tricolon or triplet.

Take these three lines from Psalm 29:

> Ascribe to the Lord, O mighty ones,
> ascribe to the Lord glory and strength.
> Ascribe to the Lord the glory due to his name.

Here the lines build up a crescendo – 'Ascribe to the Lord' is the refrain – and then different words are added in three lines.
  Or consider Psalm 3:

> O Lord, how many are my foes!
> How many rise up against me!
> Many are saying of me, 'God will not deliver him.'

Here we have the repetition of 'many', and each line builds on the previous one: who he is complaining about, what they do, then what they say. Sometimes there's an omission and a word is not included or a phrase drops out.

Other features of Hebrew poetry

Simile

Hebrew poetry is full of similes – that is, pictures that show us how one thing resembles another. For example :

> As a father has compassion on his children,
>   so the Lord has compassion on those who fear him.
>
> *from Psalm 103*

Here a tender father's care for his children is likened to God's care for his people.

Chiasm

Here the second part of the first line becomes the first part of the second line. For example:

For the Lord watches over the way of the righteous,
but the way of the wicked will perish.

from Psalm 1

The second line reverses the first – 'the way' has swapped places.

Omission

In omission (or ellipsis), part of the second line is omitted. For example:

You have put me in the lowest pit,
in the darkest depths.

from Psalm 88

We are meant to read this as if the phrase 'you have put me' recurs in the second line.

Staircase

Sometimes the lines of a psalm resemble a staircase:

The voice of the Lord breaks the cedars;
the Lord breaks in pieces the cedars of Lebanon.

from Psalm 29

The second line expands on what the first line has already told us. We already knew that 'the Lord breaks the cedars'; now we are told that he breaks them 'in pieces' and that they are cedars 'of Lebanon'.

Acrostic

Here the poetry is based on the alphabet. In Psalm 119 – the longest of all the psalms, with 176 verses – each section (and every verse in that section) begins with a new letter of the Hebrew alphabet.

Refrain

Here the second line provides a refrain throughout. For example, in Psalm 136 the words 'His love endures forever' form the second line of every verse.

Poetry in God's Word

Our study of Hebrew poetry shows us how appropriate it is that it should be included within God's Word.

Modern chorus writers have found the Psalms rich in inspiration. But when psalms are used verbatim, it is rare that a whole psalm is included. Thus we do not have the words in their original context. This can mean that the balance of the psalm is lost and, in some cases, the meaning is changed.

Hebrew poetry is easy to translate into other languages because its emphasis is on content rather than sound. If I quote English poetry when preaching to a non-English-speaking congregation through a translator, the translation kills the poem dead, because English poetry is often based on sound, and those English sounds will not survive the translation process. But Hebrew poetry can be translated into any language, so it is easy to see why God chose such a medium.

Poetry in worship

Many people argue that we should be spontaneous in our approach to God and that it is artificial for us to plan what we are going to say. There is some truth in that, but there is enormous value in first thinking through what we wish to say. The Psalms give us a model of how to address God so that we are not over-familiar, and they powerfully reveal to us God's greatness and majesty. On the other hand, they also describe an intimate relationship with God that many people may not yet have enjoyed, and so they can spur us on to seek a greater experience of God's goodness.

The planned wording that we find in biblical poetry is a necessary part of our corporate worship. If we merely sang what we wanted to sing when we came to worship, it would be chaos – not to mention a dreadful noise! Corporate worship is made possible because choruses and hymns are designed for a congregation to sing them. Those who argue that we should only sing what we 'feel' forget that there is value in voicing responses that we may *not* feel, as an encouragement to respond genuinely and also to remember the truth for the future.

There used to be a family tradition in our house. Our three children used to come and wake me up at an ungodly hour on a certain day in the year, and then stand in a row at the foot of my bed and address me in a most artificial way with poetry. They finished by giving me a bag of their favourite sweets. The poem (or song) was 'Happy birthday to you'!

Of course, in a sense this was artificial – three children standing in a row, all saying the same thing. Wouldn't it have been nicer if each of them had come separately and told me what they really felt? No, because they would then not have been doing it together as my family. The fact that they came to me together and sang to me together – in a relationship with one another – made the little tradition much more special to me.

In a similar way, it pleases the Lord when we say something together, even though we have to use words that someone else has written. God loves to see us together. We may be standing in a row, singing to God in a somewhat artificial way, but we are corporately expressing our love for God. Poetry enables us to do this.

We noted earlier that psalms lend themselves to antiphonal singing, where choirs sing to each other. It is also possible to shout psalms as well as sing them. Psalm 147 is an example of this.

Psalms can also aid our sense of corporate identity. Psalms using the words 'I' and 'my' are best for private worship, but those using 'we' and 'our' remind us that we are praising together as the whole family of God.

Just as poetry touches the heart of man, it also touches the heart of God. We have noted that poetry is used in all the Psalms and also in many of the prophetic books. The Holy Spirit chose this form as a way of communicating the mind of God and as a means for us to respond to him. Those who are sceptical about the idea that poetry touches God's heart need to remember the bold language that Scripture uses to talk of God's feelings.

For example, Psalm 2 says that God 'laughs' when he views the futile attempts of humanity to defy him. Zephaniah 3 tells us that God 'rejoices' over us 'with singing'. So God is musical! Music is not something that modern people have invented but is part of what it means to be made in the image of God.

So when God addresses us with poetry we know that he is communicating his feelings from his heart to our hearts, and so we can ask what such biblical passages tell us about God's feelings. Understanding Hebrew poetry can be a key to understanding the very heart of God.

PART I

PSALMS

tells us that God is able to do the same for us, even when our tears are about things not nearly as serious as death.

The Psalms cover the whole gamut of human emotions. They include what we might term the 'negative' emotions of anger, frustration, jealousy, despair, fear and envy. The psalmist expresses exactly how he thinks and feels, including cursing men and complaining about God. They also reflect the more 'positive' emotions of joy, excitement, hope and peace.

David wrote most of the personal psalms. They cover many of the things that people might want to say to God. Later we shall look at three particular kinds of psalms, which I call 'please psalms', 'thank-you psalms' and 'sorry psalms'.

In spite of their strong worship focus, the Psalms were not intended to be used only by priests. There is an almost complete absence of altars, priests, vestments and incense. The Psalms are intended for common people to use in their worship of God.

Biblical themes

The Psalms not only cover every human emotion; they are also comprehensive in their treatment of biblical themes. Luther said the Psalms are 'the Bible within the Bible' – the Bible in miniature. They cover the history of Israel, creation, the patriarchs, the Exodus, the monarchy, the Exile and the return to Jerusalem.

The Psalms are the most quoted Old Testament book in the New Testament. The most quoted verse in the New Testament is Psalm 110:1: 'The Lord says to my Lord: "Sit at my right hand until I make your enemies a footstool for your feet."'

Not all the psalms in the Old Testament are in the Book of Psalms. Moses and Miriam wrote one (see Exodus 15). Deborah and Hannah also composed psalms (see Judges 5 and 1 Samuel 2).

Since the authors of most of the Bible were male, it is interesting that women too wrote psalms, perhaps reflecting the naturally intuitive side of the feminine nature. Job wrote three psalms, while Isaiah and King Hezekiah each wrote one.

Other Old Testament characters also used psalms. Jonah's prayer while he was inside the whale is a classic example. He said he was praying from Sheol, the world of departed spirits, and quoted five different psalms in that prayer. Habakkuk quotes from the Psalms three times in his prophecy.

All the Psalms employ poetry as their sole means of expression. So do the Song of Solomon, Proverbs and Lamentations. Other Old Testament books (e.g. Ecclesiastes and the Prophets) are a mixture of poetry and prose. Parts of the historical books are also in poetic form (e.g. Genesis 49; Exodus 15; Judges 5; 2 Samuel 22).

Five books in one

The Book of Psalms is actually five hymn-books grouped together. Some commentators have seen parallels with the five books of the Law, but the reason why there are five books may be more mundane than that – perhaps the psalms were originally written down on five scrolls.

There is enormous variety in length among the Psalms. The shortest, Psalm 117, has only three verses, while the longest, Psalm 119, has 176 verses.

Since they were all written in Hebrew poetry, they are best read aloud. They can't be analysed in the way one might read one of Paul's epistles, focusing on each verse. Indeed, over-analysis of the Psalms serves to destroy their beauty. It is far better to read the whole psalm, meditate on it, let it sink in and, if necessary, repeat the process.

Each of the five books ends with a doxology, (see Psalms 41, 72, 89 and 106). The last book ends with Psalm 150, which is a doxology that rounds off all five books. The size of the books varies because of the different sizes of the psalms themselves, but the first book and the last book are the biggest.

Divine names

Many commentators have looked for distinguishing features in each book. There is an interesting pattern in how God is addressed within the five books. Two names are used – *Yahweh* and *Elohim* – names that appear throughout the Old Testament.

Elohim simply means 'God', though being plural it contains within it the idea of God's trinitarian nature. *Yahweh* was the personal name for God that God told Israel to use, and it is derived from the verb 'to be'. The English word 'always' conveys its meaning very well.

Yahweh is the name for God that is used mainly in Book 1. It is used on 272 occasions and *Elohim* is used on only 15. But in Book 2 the opposite is the case: – *Elohim* is used on 207 occasions and *Yahweh* on just 74. Book 3 also favours *Elohim* (36 occasions) rather than *Yahweh* (13). Books 4 and 5 switch back in favour of *Yahweh* again, with 339 *Yahweh* references and only 7 for *Elohim*.

It is not difficult to discover why this is so. King David's psalms are mostly in Books 1 and 2, with a few in Book 5. We will see later that his psalms are more personal and so use God's personal name.

The name *Elohim* communicates to us the transcendence of God. He is far removed, completely different to us; he is the Most High God. The name *Yahweh* conveys a greater sense of intimacy with God. God is both transcendent and immanent, and we need to keep both these aspects of God's nature in tension. The Psalms reflect this in the names that they ascribe to God. They begin and end with the intimate name that he revealed to his people.

Groups of psalms

Aside from the divine names, scholars have searched in vain for any system of classification in the Book of Psalms. There are groups of psalms that seem to fit together, but there is no logical order and no apparent reason why particular psalms are arranged as they are in a particular book.

The groups of psalms are as follows:

- Psalms 22–24: Saviour, shepherd and sovereign.
- Psalms 42–49: by the sons of Korah.
- Psalms 73–83: by the sons of Asaph.
- Psalms 96–99: God is king.
- Psalms 113–118: the 'hallel psalms' (sung at Passover).
- Psalms 120–134: the 'songs of ascents' (as pilgrims went 'up' to Jerusalem).
- Psalms 146–150: the 'hallelujah psalms'.

Some psalms contain parts that are repeated in other psalms (see, for example, Psalm 108 and Psalm 57:8–12).

Who wrote the Psalms?

David wrote over half the Psalms: 73 of them have his name attached to them, and the New Testament also attributes Psalms 2 and 95 to him. It is likely that others too came from his pen.

He had many roles – shepherd, warrior, king and musician – but it was this latter role that meant the most to him, for when he died he thanked God that he had been Israel's 'sweet singer'. It was the composition and singing of psalms that was closest to his heart. This ministry of David had been used in his early life to soothe Saul's troubled mind. The prophet Amos, writing centuries later, selects this image of David strumming on his harp to make a point about the complacency of Israel (see Amos 6:5).

Solomon also wrote some psalms: Psalm 72 and Psalm 127. The former was composed when the Temple was being built. He recognizes that unless the Lord builds the house, the labourers labour in vain. Without God's glory the Temple is nothing.

The sons of Korah wrote 10 psalms. A man named Korah features in a story recorded in the Book of Numbers. God punished him with death when he led a rebellion against Moses and Aaron. But generations later, his descendants were engaged in Temple worship. Their psalms appear in Book 2.

The sons of Asaph wrote 12 psalms, found in Book 3. Both they and the sons of Korah were part of the choir that served in the Temple. Since choir-masters were thought of as seers or prophets, it is no surprise that they composed some of the Psalms.

Quite a lot of the Psalms are anonymous, but they are all in Books 4 and 5. It is thought that Ezra the priest may have been responsible for Psalms 49 and 50.

A personal experience

Many of the Psalms were inspired by a personal experience, rather in the way that songs and choruses come to be written today. David had learned to sing and to play musical instruments while working as a shepherd in the countryside, and so he was used to turning his daily experiences into song.

In fact, the main parts of David's life are depicted in the Book of Psalms. For example, Psalm 3 was written after his humiliating flight from his son Absalom, who had seized the throne and forced David to flee from the palace. Psalm 7 was written about a Benjamite called Kush. Psalm 18 was written when David was delivered 'from the hand of all his enemies and from the hand of Saul'.

David wrote two penitential psalms after committing specific sins. One of them is Psalm 51, written after he had seduced Bathsheba, another man's wife, breaking five of the Ten Commandments in the process. The other was written after he had numbered his troops, an activity designed purely to boost his ego. When he realized the sin he had committed he wrote the very moving Psalm 30.

Other psalms are associated with particular places. For example, many were written by David when he was on the run from Saul at En Gedi. He often describes God as his 'rock' and 'fortress', perhaps because he hid at the huge outcrop of rock known as Masada.

Fourteen psalms have historical titles linking them to events in David's life:

- Psalm 3: When David fled from the army of his son Absalom.
- Psalm 30: David's sin prior to the dedication of the Temple area.
- Psalm 51: After Nathan exposed David's sin with Bathsheba.
- Psalm 56: David's fear at Gath.
- Psalm 57: At En Gedi, when Saul is trapped.
- Psalm 59: David's jealous associates.

- Psalm 60: The dangerous campaign in Edom.
- Psalm 63: David's flight eastwards.
- Psalm 142: David at Adullum.

Furthermore, many of the Psalms, while not including any particular details, clearly come out of David's varied experiences as musician, shepherd, fighter, refugee and king. For example, Psalm 23 is based on his daily life as a shepherd. Psalm 29 was clearly inspired by a violent thunderstorm, which reminded David of the voice of God.

David is refreshingly honest in his writing. He curses men, complains about God and asks for revenge on his enemies. But each negative comment is made to God. He tells God exactly how he feels and what he thinks, however inappropriate the emotion may seem. It is no surprise that his psalms have had such universal appeal, as people of all nations and all generations have identified with his words.

For the whole people of God

Not all the Psalms are personal; some are for the whole people of God. David wrote Psalm 2 for Solomon's coronation. It expresses David's hopes for his son, and the fulfilment of the promise that God had made to David: 'You are my Son; today I have become your Father'.

Other psalms express how a group or nation may be feeling. The 'songs of ascents' (Psalms 120–134) are appropriate for those who are on pilgrimage to Jerusalem.

Many of the Psalms are meant to help people in their personal walk with God. For example, Psalm 119 is written to encourage us to read the Bible. In every verse of that psalm there is a synonym for the Scriptures. It speaks of 'the law of the Lord', or 'the commands of the Lord', or 'the precepts of the Lord', or 'the decrees of the Lord', or 'the statutes of the Lord'.

Psalm 92 encourages the observance of the Sabbath. It teaches worshippers to proclaim God's 'love in the morning' and his 'faithfulness at night', which was the origin of morning and evening worship on a Sunday. (This has largely disappeared – now it's an hour and a half in the morning, and the rest of the day is your own!)

Actually, of course, we are not under the Sabbath law now – that is part of the law of Moses. For us every day is the Lord's day, though we are free to make one day 'special' if we wish (see Romans 14).

A 'psalm sandwich'

Psalms 22–24 form a very important group. They are like a sandwich, though people tend to lick the jam out and leave the bread! Let me explain. These psalms really belong together – I call them the cross, the crook and the crown. They present us with a Lord who is first of all Saviour, then Shepherd, and then Sovereign. If we just extract the well-known Psalm 23 from the middle of the 'sandwich' and claim that Jesus is our shepherd, we miss the lessons of the two psalms on either side of it.

Psalm 22 begins with the cry that Jesus would later quote from the cross: 'My God, my God, why have you forsaken me?' Whereas Psalm 23 begins: 'The Lord is my shepherd.' The order of the two psalms implies that until we have been to the cross and found the Lord as our Saviour, we are not able to regard him as our Shepherd.

Psalm 24 then says: 'Who is this King of glory? The Lord strong and mighty, the Lord mighty in battle. Lift up your heads, O you gates; lift them up, you ancient doors, that the King of glory may come in' (verses 8–9). Or, to paraphrase: 'Open up the gates – the Lord is coming as our Sovereign, our King of Kings, our Lord of Lords.' So we only have Jesus as the Good Shepherd because he was first our Saviour and is our coming King.

Those three psalms fit so beautifully together. In a book that I produced called *Loose Leaves from the Bible* I translated them into modern English:

> My God, my God, why?
> Why have you left me all alone – me, of all people?
> Why do you seem so distant,
>   too far away to help me
>   or even to hear my groans?
> O my God, I shout in the daylight,
>   but there's no reply from you;
> I howl in the dark,
>   but no relief comes.
> It doesn't make sense,
>   because you are utterly good,
>   lauded to the skies by this nation.
> Our ancestors trusted you to the hilt;
>   and when they did,
>   you got them out of trouble.
> They appealed to you –
>   and reached safety;
> when they relied on you
>   they were never let down.
> But I am treated more like a worm than a human being,
>   with no consideration from men
>   and only contempt from the mob.
> Everyone looking at me makes fun of me;

> they put their tongues out,
>   shrug their shoulders and jeer:
> 'He said the Lord would prove him right;
>   see if he gets him out of this!
> If the Lord is so fond of him,
>   let him set him free.'
> If they only knew –
>   you were the one who brought me safely through
>   childbirth
>   and you kept me safe while I was still being breast-fed.
>   I have had to depend on you
>   since my life began;
> and you have been my very own God
>   since my mother brought me into the world.
>   Don't leave me now when I'm in such peril,
>   for there is no-one else who can possibly help.
> I'm in a bull-ring,
>   surrounded by the most ferocious beasts in the whole
>   country;
>   they bare their teeth, like a fierce, famished lion.
> My strength is draining away,
>   my joints are being dislocated,
>   my heart beats like putty in my chest,
>   my body is as dry as baked clay,
>   my tongue is stuck to the roof of my mouth.
> You're letting me disintegrate into dead dust.
> A gang of crooks circle me like a pack of hounds;
>   they've already torn my hands and my feet.
> My bones stand out clear enough to count,
>   but they just stare and gloat over me.
> They've grabbed my clothes
>   and they're gambling for my shirt.
> What do you think you're doing, Lord?

Don't remain aloof!
You're my only support!
Hurry back to my side!
Save my dear life from this violent end –
from the fangs of the dogs,
from the jaws of these lions,
from the horns of these bulls ...
You've given me your answer!

I'll tell my brothers you've lived up to your name again;
I'll be among them when they meet and share my testimony.
Each one of you who fears this God Jehovah,
tell him how much you think of him.
Everyone who claims to be descended from Jacob,
give all the credit to him.
All who belong to the nation of Israel,
hold him in deep respect.
For he was neither too haughty or too horrified
to get involved with the suffering of the underdog;
he didn't turn his back on him,
but listened to his cry for help.
You will give your praise to me
in the large congregation;
and I will keep the promises I made to you,
as reverent eyes will see.
Those who suffered will be satisfied;
those who have been seekers will become singers.
May this thrilling experience last for ever.
In every corner of the world,
people will think about God again
and come back to him.
Different races and nations
will be really united

in worshipping him.
For the Lord controls the world
    and is in charge of all international affairs.
Yes, even the top people will bow to his superiority,
    for they are but mortals heading for the grave
    and nobody can hold on to his life indefinitely.
Future generations will take over his work,
    for men will talk about this God who really exists
    to their children who come after them.
His liberation will be announced
    to those whose lives haven't even started yet;
they will be told that God has worked it all out
    and it is finished!

Psalm 22

This Psalm was clearly in Jesus' mind as he died on the cross.

The only God who really exists,
    the God of the Jews
cares for me as an individual,
    like a shepherd for his sheep;
so that I'll never lack anything
    that I really need.
He forces me to rest,
    where there is abundant nourishment;
then he moves me on,
    making sure I have constant refreshment.
He puts new life into me
    when I'm exhausted.
He keeps me on the right track,
    to maintain his good reputation.
Even if I travel through a deep, dark ravine,
    where danger lurks in the shadows,

I'm not afraid of coming to any harm,
     because you are right there beside me.
With your cudgel to guard and your crook to guide,
     I feel quite safe.
You lay the table for me,
     in full view of my helpless foes;
you treat me as an honoured guest
     and put on a lavish spread.
For the rest of my days nothing will chase after me –
     except your generous and undeserved kindness
and I'll be at home with this God,
     as long as I live.

Psalm 23

The God of the Jews owns this planet,
     with everything in it
     and everyone on it;
because he built up the land from the bed of the ocean
     and sent down the water that flows in its rivers.
But who could scale his holy height?
     And who could stay in his perfect presence?
Only one whose conduct was faultless
     and whose character was flawless;
who had not based his life on things that don't ring true
     and who had never broken his word.
Such a man would be given attention and approval
     by the God who saved him.
For people like this really want to find God
     and meet him face to face, as Jacob did.

(Pause for a moment and think about yourself.)

Fling wide the city gates!
  Open up the old citadel doors!
His magnificent Majesty is about to enter!
Who is this marvellous monarch?
  The powerful God of the Jews,
  the undefeated God of Israel!
Fling wide the city gates!
  Open up those old citadel doors!
His magnificent Majesty is about to enter!
Who is this marvellous monarch?
  The God who commands all the forces of the universe –
that's who this marvellous monarch is!

(Be quiet for a while and think about him.)

Psalm 24

God is King

We can deal with the other groups of psalms with greater brevity.

Psalms 96–99 have a common theme: God is King. This is the nearest we get in the Old Testament to the concept of the kingdom of God.

Psalms 113–118 are known in Hebrew as the 'hallel psalms' and are sung together at the Passover.

Psalm 118 provided the inspiration for a well-known modern chorus: 'This is the day that the Lord has made,/We will rejoice and be glad in it.' However, 'the day' being referred to is actually the Passover day in the Old Testament, not Sunday or any other day.

Also in Psalm 118 is the cry, 'O Lord, save us', or literally, 'liberate us'. The Hebrew for 'liberate us' is *ho shanah*, from which we get the word 'hosanna'.

Unfortunately, we now think of it as a kind of heavenly 'hello'! It is actually a demand for freedom. When Jesus rode into Jerusalem on a donkey the people saying 'Hosanna!' were actually calling for him to liberate them from the Romans. The crowd fell silent because he took a whip and drove out the Jewish businessmen from the Temple instead of attacking the Romans.

Psalms 120–134 are called the 'songs of ascent', meaning 'songs of going up'. Jerusalem is, of course, right up at the top of the hills (actually, it is in a little hollow at the top), so all the pilgrims had to go up to Jerusalem.

Psalm 121 means a great deal to my wife and I, because some years ago she had cancer in her eye and was in danger of losing her life. The surgeons were battling for her life, and I was wondering what to preach on that Sunday while she was in hospital. The Lord directed me to Psalm 121, and I found that every verse is about eyes. The first line is 'I will lift up my eyes to the hills.' When walking up to Jerusalem it is a very danger-ous thing not to keep your eyes on your feet, but the psalmist says, 'I will lift up my eyes to the hills.' So I preached on that psalm and took a tape recording of it to her in hospital. However, a young nurse, who had only been a Christian for two months, had already beaten me to it. She had visited my wife and had given her a word from the Lord: 'You will lift up your eyes to the hills.' A few weeks later we were in Canada and climbing the Rockies together. She has had no trace of cancer since then.

The final group is Psalms 146–150. They are all 'Hallelujah!' songs. *Hallelujah* is Hebrew for 'Praise the Lord' (*hallele* means 'praise' and *Jah* is a short form of *Yahweh*).

Types of psalm

Although it is not possible to classify the books of psalms, there are a number of types of psalm that we can identify.

Lament psalms

First, there are the lament psalms or 'please psalms'. They are sad songs written out of the personal unhappiness of the psalmist. In some he is ill; in others he has suffered injustice; in a few he feels his own guilt. Many people are surprised to discover that, with 42 lament psalms, this category is larger than any other.

There is a lot of self-pity in these psalms, but the feelings are presented to God, and healing is found.

They all have the same form and would have been sung to slow funereal music. They each have five parts:

1 A cry to God.
2 A complaint about what is wrong.
3 A confession of trust that God will deliver.
4 A petition calling on God to intervene.
5 A promise to praise God when deliverance comes.

All the lament psalms follow this five-fold pattern. This is why it is necessary to read the whole psalm – just a few verses from a psalm don't give the whole form.

If you just took the first bit, then you would wallow in self-pity. But the psalmist always finishes by promising to praise God when he is out of the situation.

While most of these are individual psalms, some were written on behalf of the nation (see Psalms 44, 74, 79, 80, 83, 85 and 90). Interestingly, none of these were written by David.

Psalms of gratitude

Secondly, there are the psalms of gratitude. These 'thank-you psalms' are the largest group after the lament psalms. They have a particular form and almost all of them are anonymous. Four things are said in every one of them:

1 A proclamation: 'I am going to praise ...'
2 A statement about what he is going to praise God for.
3 A testimony of deliverance.
4 A vow of praise: he continues to praise God for what has happened.

These psalms say a lot about God's attributes and activity. They contain thanks for God's kingly rule, for the creation, for the Exodus, for Jerusalem, for the Temple, and for the opportunity to engage in pilgrimage. There is also gratitude for God's Word, seen supremely in the 176 verses of Psalm 119.

Psalms of penitence

Thirdly, there are the psalms of penitence or 'sorry psalms'. They are few in number but reflect the deep contrition felt when the psalmist is made aware of his sin. Note especially Psalms 6, 32, 38, 51, 130 and 143.

Special psalms

There are also certain other special categories of psalm.

Royal psalms

Just as David wrote about his experiences as a shepherd, he also wrote from his experiences as a king. Psalms 2, 18, 20, 21,

45, 72, 89, 101, 110, 132 and 144 fit into this category.

The British national anthem is based on a number of these psalms. Psalm 68 focuses on the king's victory in battle, which is the background to the line 'Send her victorious' in the anthem. The big difference, of course, is that a British monarch is not the ruler of the Lord's people, so many of these statements are inappropriate. There is only one nation that God chose to be his nation, and that is Israel. We must never forget that any non-Jewish nation is a Gentile nation, and so cannot be special in the same way as Israel.

There is, however, a wonderful psalm about a queen. Psalm 45 reflects on how unworthy the queen felt to be the king's wife. This is a good picture of how we ought to feel as the bride of Christ. We are going to sit on thrones with Jesus, and live like royalty.

Many nations have thought that they were the chosen nation, and so used the Psalms wrongly. The lion and the unicorn in the English coat of arms come from Psalm 22. One of the earliest English translations of the Bible includes the unicorn, even though the word was not in the original.

Canada is the only nation in the world with 'The Dominion' in its name. The name 'The Dominion of Canada' is based on Psalm 72: 'He shall have dominion … from sea to sea' (AV). Canada stretches from the Pacific to the Atlantic and so was called the Dominion of Canada by its founding fathers.

Messianic psalms

Some of the royal psalms are also messianic or prophetic psalms. David was a model of the ideal king, and these psalms reflect the desire for a king who is truly worthy of God's honour.

The word 'Messiah' means 'anointed'. Every king of Israel was anointed with oil at his coronation as a symbol of the Holy

Spirit. Even the kings and queens of England have what is called 'the unction', the anointing with oil (a special blended oil made from 24 different herbs and oils).

The word 'Messiah' (meaning 'anointed one', as does 'Christ' in Greek) occurs only once in the whole of the Old Testament, in Psalm 2. But if the Psalms are examined for their prophetic element, we find that 20 of them are quoted in the New Testament. It is astonishing to note what is prophesied about Jesus, the Son of David, in these psalms:

■ God will declare him to be his Son.
■ God will put all things under his feet.
■ God will not let him see corruption in the grave.
■ He will be forsaken by God and scorned and mocked by men; his hands and feet will be pierced; his clothes will be gambled for; but none of his bones will be broken.
■ False witnesses will accuse him.
■ He will be hated without a cause.
■ A friend will betray him.
■ He will be given vinegar and gall to drink.
■ He will pray for his enemies.
■ His betrayer's office will be given to another.
■ His enemies will be his footstool.
■ He will be a priest after the order of Melchizedek.
■ He will be the chief cornerstone and will come in the name of the Lord.

David called himself a prophet because he could see someone else as he wrote. It is amazing how David was able to enter into the sufferings of Jesus on the cross, without ever having experienced them himself.

Psalm 22 begins, 'My God, my God, why have you forsaken me?' (the words that Jesus cried from the cross).

It speaks of pierced hands and feet centuries before the Romans used crucifixion as a method of execution. One of the greatest 'I am' statements of Jesus occurs in this Psalm, and is very unexpected: – 'I am a worm and not a man'.

Wisdom psalms

The 'wisdom psalms' are the result of quiet reflection and meditation. They resemble the Book of Proverbs, and are full of practical wisdom for life.

Wisdom in the Bible is concerned primarily with two things: – the conduct of life and the contradictions of life.

The Book of Psalms begins with a wisdom psalm about the conduct of life. There are two ways in which we can walk: 'the way of the wicked', or 'the way of the righteous'. Towards the end of Matthew's account of the Sermon on the Mount, Jesus uses similar words: 'For wide is the gate and broad is the road that leads to destruction, and many enter through it. But small is the gate and narrow the road that leads to life, and only a few find it'. So Psalm 1 implies that this Book of Psalms is for those who are walking in the right way. It is not for those who sit, walk or stand with the evildoers. If we walk with someone, we pick up something from them. If we stand around with them, the relationship is getting deeper. If we sit with them we become friends. We read that we must not walk, stand or sit in the way of sinners, because the company we keep is probably the biggest influence in our life.

The wisdom psalms also focus on the contradictions of life. The biggest contradiction is that bad people often get away with their evil behaviour while good people suffer.

Psalm 73 tackles this problem head on. The psalmist feels as if he has cleansed his heart in vain, that it is a waste of time trying to live a good life, because wicked people die in their beds in peace, having made plenty of money.

The psalmist says he is troubled all the day and can't sleep at night. His solution is to go to the Temple and reflect on God's glory and the end that the wicked will face. It is one of the few psalms that mention the afterlife. The concept of the afterlife isn't explained as thoroughly in the Old Testament as it is in the New.

Imprecatory psalms

In these psalms the psalmists ask God to visit their enemies with judgement.

For example:

> Let the heads of those who surround me
> be covered with the trouble their lips have caused.
>   Let burning coals fall upon them;
> may they be thrown into the fire,
> into miry pits, never to rise.
>
> *from Psalm 140*

One of the best known imprecatory psalms is Psalm 137, which was composed in Babylon:

> By the rivers of Babylon we sat and wept
> when we remembered Zion.
> There on the poplars
> we hung our harps,
> for there our captors asked us for songs,
> our tormentors demanded songs of joy;
> they said, 'Sing us one of the songs of Zion!'
>
> How can we sing the songs of the Lord
> while in a foreign land?
> If I forget you, O Jerusalem,

may my right hand forget its skill.
May my tongue cling to the roof of my mouth
if I do not remember you,
if I do not consider Jerusalem my highest joy.

Remember, O Lord, what the Edomites did
on the day Jerusalem fell.
'Tear it down,' they cried,
'tear it down to its foundations!'

O Daughter of Babylon, doomed to destruction,
happy is he who repays you
for what you have done to us –
he who seizes your infants
and dashes them against the rocks.

This is not pleasant. There is no forgiveness for the enemy and certainly no recognition that what is being said might be inappropriate. It is understandable that some people should ask whether Christians should use these psalms at all.

Can Christians use imprecatory psalms?

First, we must remember that the Jews only had the Old Testament. Hence, we mustn't expect the Old Testament to feel fully Christian. They had no knowledge of Jesus, who said, 'Father, forgive them, for they do not know what they are doing'.

Secondly, these psalms are good models of honesty in prayer. If we feel a certain way, then it is appropriate to tell God how we feel. It is just as bad to feel the way the psalmist does and not say it, as it is to say it. In fact it is worse, because we are trying to hide it from God.

I remember a Christian lady who had been in a terrible car crash. For 20 years afterwards she was dreadfully handicapped; she could only stagger around on crutches and was in constant pain. One night, as she was going into her bedroom, she cursed God for her agony. But then she caught her foot on the carpet and fell over, knocking herself out. She was unconscious for many hours, and when she woke up it was morning, and sunlight was coming through the window and shining directly into her eyes. She was convinced that she had died and was now facing the Lord, and with horror she remembered that the last thing she had done in life had been to curse God. She assumed that she would have to go to hell because of this. But then she realized that the bright light was in fact just sunshine and she was still in her bedroom. The relief was enormous. Then she suddenly noticed that she had no pain. She got up and discovered that she was totally healed. She could move every limb! She dashed out into the street and told everybody she met that she had cursed God but he had made her well! Of course, this is not a good model to copy, but the point is that because she was honest with God, this lady received healing from him. How gracious he is!

Thirdly, the enemies of Israel were also God's enemies. The imprecatory psalms do not just ask for vengeance on the psalmists' personal enemies; they also remind God that the psalmists' enemies are His enemies. For Christians today, the enemies of God are not flesh and blood, but the principalities and powers. If we really love God, we will hate the devil and all evil. The Old Testament saints did not have the knowledge that we have about the Day of Judgement and heaven and hell, so they had to pray that the wicked would be punished in this present world. They believed that after death everyone went to a place called Sheol – a kind of railway station waiting-room where no trains arrive. They had to pray for God to be vindicated in this life. They were crying to a good God for justice.

Fourthly, in every case the psalmists refuse to take revenge themselves, but leave it to God. This is a principle that Paul teaches in Romans 12: 'Do not take revenge, my friends, but leave room for God's wrath'. He will take vengeance on the wicked.

Finally, it is important to note that in this matter the New Testament is no different from the Old. There are also imprecatory prayers in the New Testament. In Revelation 6 the souls of the martyrs in heaven are praying, 'How long, Sovereign Lord, holy and true, until you judge the inhabitants of the earth and avenge our blood?'. These prayers are no different from the imprecatory psalms, even though they are made 'in heaven'. The Christian martyrs are asking God to vindicate himself and to bring justice.

So if we do it in the right spirit, we have no problem using these psalms today. One day every sin will be punished, the righteous will be vindicated and the martyrs will sit on the very thrones that condemned them to death.

The Psalms' view of God

The Psalms are remarkably balanced in their view of God. We have already seen how his transcendence (*Elohim*) is balanced by his immanence (*Yahweh*).

The Psalms encourage us to magnify God, not because we can make him bigger, but so that our view of him may be enlarged.

The Psalms tell us about God's *attributes* – that is, what he *is*. Psalms 8, 9, 29, 103, 104, 139, 148 and 150 are good examples of this. Psalm 139 describes his omnipotence (i.e. he is all-powerful), his omniscience (he is all-knowing) and his omnipresence (he is everywhere).

The Psalms also tell us about God's *actions* – that is, what he *does*. Psalms 33, 36, 105, 111, 113, 117, 136, 146 and 147 are good examples of this. In particular we learn about his two major acts:

> *creation* (e.g. Psalms 8 and 19) and
> *redemption* (e.g. Psalm 78, which tells the story of the Exodus).

The Psalms tell us that God is Shepherd, Warrior, Judge, Father and, above all, King.

In view of these attributes and actions of God, it is no surprise that in the Psalms theology very quickly becomes doxology. Truth leads inevitably to praise.

Using the Psalms today

It is clear from the New Testament's use of the Psalms that it is legitimate and desirable for Christians to use them. The songs in the New Testament are modelled on the Psalms (e.g. Luke chapters 1 and 2). The apostles turn to the Psalms when they are under pressure (e.g. Acts 4), and they often use them when they are preaching (e.g. Acts 13).

The writer of the Letter to the Hebrews quotes the Psalms extensively. Each of the first five chapters of Hebrews includes a reference to one or more psalms.

Jesus quoted from the Psalms in his public teaching (e.g. the Sermon on the Mount), in answering the Jews, while cleansing the Temple and at the Last Supper.

So how should the Psalms be used today?

It is best if they are read aloud or sung. Some of them explicitly encourage shouting! Their impact and value is greatly diminished if they are read silently. Many psalms also encourage bodily movement such as lifting hands, clapping, dancing and looking upwards.

We are commanded in the New Testament to use the Psalms in corporate worship (e.g. Ephesians 5). They can be sung or read aloud to the congregation by singers or readers, or the whole congregation can read, sing (or even shout!) them together.

Clearly the Psalms are meant to be sung to musical accompaniment. As we have already seen, the Hebrew word that we translate as 'psalm' literally means 'pluck', implying that stringed instruments normally accompanied the singing of psalms (though other instruments are also mentioned in the Book of Psalms). In many psalms the word *Selah* occurs. It is probably a musical direction to the choir-master meaning 'pause' or 'change key' or 'play louder' or even 'lift up your voices at this point'.

How should we sing psalms today? I think they should be sung 'whole'. Too many songs, choruses and hymns use only parts of a psalm, and in doing so they violate its original sense and context.

Some psalms can be sung in metrical verse (as is often done in churches in Scotland). Some psalms are well suited to being sung by a choir. The Psalms are also well suited to private use. Here are some guidelines:

- Reading one psalm per day is a good habit.
- Some psalms are ideal bedtime reading. They can be a help against destructive emotions and bad dreams.
- Read psalms even when they don't seem to be relevant to your circumstances, because there will come a time when they will be.
- Try giving a title to the psalm – this will help you to concentrate on its content.
- Translate the psalm into your own words. (See my examples earlier in the chapter.)

■ Some psalms are a great comfort when you are ill – or even
  when you are dying.

While there is great value in studying the Psalms, we derive
the greatest benefit from them as we *use* them in our lives.
We discover their true beauty and power when we read them
aloud, sing them, and shout them. The Psalms are meant to
lead us into a passionate praise that glorifies God.

PART II

SONG OF SONGS

Introduction

Many people are surprised to find the Song of Songs included in the Bible. It is one of only two books in the Bible where God is not mentioned even once (Esther is the other). There is no mention of anything obviously spiritual in it from beginning to end, and its graphic description of human sexuality means that it's one of the books of the Bible that are generally avoided during Sunday school!

The very title 'Song of Songs' sounds strange. Hebrew writing does not include any adjectives, so phrases such as 'fantastic song' or 'brilliant song' are not possible. So instead of 'the Greatest Song', the expression 'the Song of Songs' is used, just as 'the Highest King' is known as 'the King of Kings' and 'the Greatest Lord' is called 'the Lord of Lords'.

But accepting that it is a lovely song gives us no clear understanding of why it is in the Bible, for not only is it unspiritual, but it is also very sensual. It touches all five senses – smell, sight, touch, taste and hearing – and gives an erotic description of the bodies of the young man and the young woman in the drama. So although it is not taught at Sunday school, it becomes something of a favourite with young people!

For many years I didn't preach from this book because I didn't know how to handle it. But I found that the Jewish Rabbis treated it as a very holy book. They called it 'the Holy

of Holies' and even took off their shoes when they read it.
Furthermore, I learnt that some Christian devotional writers
raved about it. I determined to get to grips with it for myself,
and so I bought commentaries and devotional expositions of the
book in order to gain some understanding of it. But this just
increased my sense of guilt. I was told that the book was written
in a hidden code and that none of the words meant what I
thought they meant. I reached rock bottom when I read one
commentary's explanation of a verse in chapter 1 where the
woman in the drama speaks of her lover resting between her
breasts, and the commentator said that this means between the
Old and the New Testaments! I confess that this was the last
thing in my mind when I read that verse, and so I concluded that
God must have put this book in the Bible as a kind of 'Catch 22'
to find out whether you were spiritual or carnal. It was many
years before I was able to explore the book in any depth.

What sort of literature is it?

Allegory?

An allegory is a fictional story that is intended to communicate a hidden message. For example, *The Pilgrim's Progress*, the
seventeenth-century classic by John Bunyan, is an allegory in
which each part of the story is intended to depict a spiritual
truth. Many have interpreted the Song of Songs as an allegory,
but each commentator seems to invent his or her own code,
often with little reference to the text itself. It seems that the
commentators see what they want to see and are reluctant to
take the plain meaning of the text, because they don't believe
that the book, with its graphic descriptions of sexuality, is
acceptable as it stands.

One reason for this is that Christians have generally been

more influenced by Greek thinking than by Hebrew thinking.
The Greeks believed that life was divided between what they
termed 'the physical' and 'the spiritual', with the latter regarded as more important. By contrast, the Hebrews believed in
one God who made both the physical and the spiritual, and
they saw no difference in value between the two. If a good God
made this material world, then material things are good; and if
this same God made us male and female, with the capacity to
fall in love and become man and wife, this too was good.

Affirmation

This Hebrew way of thinking can help us in our interpretation
of the book, for, rather than seeing the book as an allegory, we
should see it instead as affirmation. Here in the middle of the
Bible, God is affirming the love between a man and a woman.
His inclusion of the Song of Songs within the Bible reminds us
that sexuality is God's idea. He thought it up. Indeed, one of
the biggest lies that the devil has spread around the world is
that God is against sex and Satan is for it. The truth is the exact
opposite. God is saying that sex is a clean and legitimate part
of a married couple's love for one another. Indeed, when con-
ducting a marriage service, I always read part of the Song
of Songs and tell the couple to read the rest of it on their
honeymoon.

Analogy

But the Song of Songs is more than affirmation – it is also an
analogy. This is clearly distinct from the fanciful allegorical
interpretations that we have discounted. An allegory is a work
of fiction with a hidden meaning, whereas an analogy is a fact
which is like another fact. Jesus used analogies in his teaching.
For example, he would describe the Kingdom of Heaven
in terms that his hearers could grasp. The Song of Songs

functions in a similar way. The love between a man and a woman is like the love between God and human beings. Both are real, and the former helps to explain the latter. The Song of Songs is saying that our relationship to God can be like that. We should be able to say, 'My beloved is mine and I am his', in the same way that lovers speak of one another.

The book's author

The book was written by King Solomon, who had a gift for writing lyrics. In 1 Kings we learn that he wrote 1,005 songs in all, though only six were included in the Bible. My theory is that Solomon wrote a song for each of his 700 wives and 300 concubines, but of all these 1,000 women, only one was God's choice for him, and so the song that he wrote for her was the only love song that was published as part of the Bible. The Song of Songs tells us that by the time he wrote the song he already had 60 wives.

Three people or two?

Scholars are divided about the plot. Some argue that it involves three people – a triangular tug of war between a shepherd boy, a king and the girl, who is torn between the two. It makes an interesting story and a good sermon, because you can finish it with a moving appeal: '*You* are that girl! Will you choose the prince of this world or the Good Shepherd?' But unfortunately this plot does not fit the text – why would Solomon compose a song depicting the king (himself) as the villain? Furthermore, the atmosphere is one of innocence, not guilt. This is not an evil king seducing a simple girl. It's a pure love song all the way through.

So it is more likely to be a plot featuring just two people, which means that the king and the shepherd are the same person. This may seem improbable until we remember that some of the kings of Israel were once shepherds – David being an obvious example. Moses too was a shepherd before he became a leader of God's people. It is not an unusual combination.

But even assuming that the king and the shepherd are one and the same, it is still not easy to understand exactly how the story fits together. It is a little like taking the lid off a jigsaw box and seeing all the different coloured pieces mixed up inside. We despair of ever finishing unless we have the picture on the lid to help us.

So let me give you the picture on the lid so that when you read the story for yourself, all the little bits will fit together.

The story

Solomon had a country estate on the slopes of Mount Hermon. He used it as a retreat from the pressures of being King in Jerusalem. He could relax, go hunting and forget for a while that he was the King. On occasions he would lead sheep to find green pasture and water amid the rocky terrain. He might typically travel 15 miles in any one day.

On Solomon's country estate a tenant farmer had died. The farm passed to his sons, though we don't know exactly how many there were. There were probably three or four sons and two daughters. One of the daughters is a child; the other is grown up and is the subject of the song. Her life lacks any excitement. Her father divided the estate, giving vineyards to the sons and daughters, but the sons make her do all the work in the house and a lot of the work on the farm. She complains that she had to look after their vineyards so much that she

neglected her own. Furthermore, because she had been working outside, her skin had become dark. Although bronzed skin
is an attractive feature in our culture, the reverse was true for
her – indeed, a bride would be kept out of the sun for 12
months before her wedding. So she was conscious of the fact
that her dark looks meant that she would probably remain a
slave to her brothers for the rest of her life.

One day she is working in the fields and meets a young
man. They enjoy conversation and arrange to meet the next
day. After a few occasional meetings, they agree to meet every
day. The meetings become the highlight of the day, and after a
fortnight they are deeply in love. The one thing that troubles
the woman is that she doesn't know who the young man is. She
keeps pestering him, asking which farm he comes from and
where he rests his sheep at midday. But he evades her questions
and will not tell her who he is.

She is deeply in love with him and he with her, and finally
he asks if she will marry him. She has waited years for this! She
is overjoyed and says 'Yes' immediately. He tells her that he has
to leave the next day to return to work in the south in the big
city. He leaves her to get ready for the wedding and promises
to return.

The next few months are the most exciting of her life. She
never thought it would happen, but now at last she is to be
married. But she begins to have nightmares. It doesn't take a
very deep knowledge of psychology to interpret her dreams.
All the dreams are centred on one theme: 'I've lost him and I'm
looking for him.'

One night she dreams that she is running through the
streets, looking for her lover. She meets the watchman and asks
whether he has seen him. But he hasn't. She runs around the
streets, frantically searching for him. When she finds him, she
gets hold of him, drags him back to her mother's bedroom and

tells him she will never let him go. When she awakes, she finds that she is holding the pillow.

Another time she dreams that her lover is at the door and puts his hand through the hole in the door to lift the latch on the inside. But he is unable to open it because it is bolted further down. She is paralysed and can't move. She can't get off the bed, and he's trying to open the door, and she becomes frustrated. Then his hand disappears and she finds that she can move. She runs to the door and – he's gone!

The nightmares have a simple explanation: she's afraid that he won't come back to marry her. She thinks this is only a holiday flirtation, and her lover won't keep his promise.

Then one day, she's out in the fields and notices horses and chariots and a great cloud of dust approaching. She asks her brothers who it is.

The brothers say it is the landlord, King Solomon from Jerusalem, who has come to visit his estates. They get ready to bow down low before the King. She has never seen him, and so she takes a look – only to find that the King in the big chariot is her young man!

Since everyone knows that he has got 60 wives already, she realizes that she must be number 61!

So she leaves the farm and travels south to live in the palace. They are married, and she appears at the first banquet, held to honour her. She sits at the top table next to the King, and feels distinctly inferior to the 60 beautiful, fair-skinned queens in their robes all around her.

When a man has more than one woman, each woman begins to feel insecure and asks whether he loves her more than the others. So she asks Solomon if they can go back north. 'Can't we just lie on the grass under the trees? Couldn't we go and live on your estate up there?' He explains that because he is the King he must live and reign in Jerusalem. Finally she asks about the beautiful women all around her. She says with a tone of real inferiority, 'I'm just a rose of Sharon, I'm a lily of the valley.'

We assume that these are beautiful flowers, but in Israel they are tiny little flowers which you would walk on like daisies in a lawn. The lilies of the valley grow in the shadows, and the rose of Sharon is a tiny little crocus that grows on the flat plain next to the Mediterranean Sea.

The King's reply, that she is a lily among thorns, delights her, for lilies among thorns, by contrast, are the most beautiful flowers in Israel. This lily is white with a graceful form, and this is how her beloved sees her. So she sings a little song to rejoice, and the song is: 'He brought me into his banqueting hall and his banner over me is love.'

This, then, is the outline of the story – the picture on the jigsaw box.

Why should we read this book?

There are two reasons why we should read it and study it. First, at the heart of Christianity is a very personal relationship. Being a Christian is not going to church, reading a Bible or supporting missionaries; being a Christian is being in love with the Lord. The only point of singing hymns is that we are singing love songs. If we miss this, we miss everything.

So at the heart of the Bible is the very intimate, loving relationship between Solomon and a country girl.

The book adds a wider dimension to the portrayal of the relationship between God and his people. Sometimes in the Bible, God is spoken of as a husband and Israel as a wife. He courts her and marries her at Sinai when the covenant is established. When Israel goes after other gods, she is described as an adulteress.

This theme underlies the prophecy of Hosea. The Lord asks the prophet to find a prostitute in the street. He protests and asks God why. He is told to marry her, and she will have three children. She will love the first child, but not the second, and the third child, who won't even be Hosea's, is to be called 'Not Mine'. God tells Hosea that she will return to life on the street in her old profession, leaving the three children with him. He is to find her, buy her back from the pimp who is controlling her and bring her back home, and then he is to love her again. Finally, God tells him to tell Israel that this is how God feels about them.

In fact, the whole relationship in the Old Testament between God and Israel is that of a husband whose wife behaves appallingly. He woos her, wins her, loses her, still loves her, and wants to get her back home again.

When we move to the New Testament, this same theme continues. Jesus is depicted as the bridegroom looking for a bride. On the last page of the Bible the bride is eager for the wedding and says 'Come!' She has made herself ready with white linen, which is righteousness. So the whole Bible is a love story from beginning to end.

The Song of Songs expresses this relationship. The words of the young man to the bride are the words that God says to us. Her replies are the sort of responses we can make. So it's not an allegory, nor is it full of hidden meanings. 'Pomegranates' means 'pomegranates' and 'breasts' mean 'breasts'. God means what he says, but it's an analogy of the relationship that we can have with God.

We need to be careful in our interpretation. Our relationship with the Lord is not erotic, but it is emotional. Even though the song includes sexually explicit language, there is appropriate restraint. It doesn't enter into the physical details that modern literature would.

Nevertheless, it is an emotional relationship. The story reminds us of the conversation between Jesus and Peter in Galilee after Jesus' resurrection. Peter had denied the Lord at a charcoal fire in a courtyard, and the only other charcoal fire mentioned in the New Testament is a few weeks later, in Galilee. So Peter sees the fire and he remembers those awful moments. Yet Jesus doesn't say how disappointed he is with him, nor does he exclude him from future service. No, he tells Peter that he can cope with him, provided that he is sure of one thing – that Peter loves him.

In the same way, the Lord doesn't ask us how many times we have been to church or how many chapters of the Bible we have read this week. He asks us: 'Do you love me?' Jesus said that the law could be summarized as: 'Love the Lord your God with all your heart and mind and strength, and love your neighbour as yourself.' Love really is as important as this.

Secondly, not only is your relationship with the Lord a very personal one; it's also a very public one. Most people fall in love with the Lord because they see him as their Shepherd, the One who will be with them in the valley of the shadow of death, the One who will lead them by the still waters and the green pastures. But at some stage after we have fallen in love with Jesus as our Shepherd, we discover that he is also a King! He's the King of Kings, and we are his bride. We are going to reign with him and become his queen. So we are in very public view, which puts an extra responsibility on us. It would be nice if we could keep it private and return to the forests of Hermon, keeping our relationship with the Lord secret. It would save a lot of unpleasantness, criticism and exposure. But he wants us to remain in the spotlight, forever pointing to him as the source of our life and sharing with him the responsibility of reigning over the earth.

PART III

PROVERBS

Introduction[1]

Proverbs seems at first to be a strange book to be included in the Bible. It contains humorous observations and pithy sayings that seem to be little more than common sense.

The book doesn't seem very spiritual. It says little about private or public devotions, and some of its themes seem distinctly mundane.

Some of the proverbs make points which are obvious to everyone. For example: 'Poverty is the ruin of the poor'; 'A happy heart makes the face cheerful'; 'Better to live on a corner of the roof than share a house with a quarrelsome wife'; 'Like one who seizes a dog by the ears is a passer-by who meddles in a quarrel not his own'.

Some of the proverbs seem more entertaining than edifying, and others seem downright immoral. For example: 'A bribe does wonders, it will bring you before men of importance'.

Many of the proverbs have found their way into everyday speech:

---

1 For Proverbs (and Ecclesiastes) I am deeply indebted to the superb commentaries of Derek Kidner in the 'Tyndale' series published by IVP. Readers wanting to study these books in greater detail are warmly commended to obtain these models of their kind.

'Spare the rod and spoil the child';
'Hope deferred makes the heart sick';
'Pride goes before a fall';
'Stolen food is sweet';
'Iron sharpens iron'.

The Book of Proverbs describes life as it really is – not life in church, but life in the street, the office, the shop, the home. The book covers all aspects of life – not just what you do on Sundays in church. It considers how you should live throughout the week in every situation.

So the characters who are found in the Book of Proverbs can be easily recognized in all cultures. There is the woman who talks too much, the wife who is always nagging, the aimless youth hanging around on street corners, the neighbour who is always dropping in and staying too long, the friend who is unbearably cheerful first thing in the morning.

Indeed, the 900 proverbs cover most of life's important subjects, often presenting them as contrasts: wisdom and folly, pride and humility, love and lust, wealth and poverty, work and leisure, masters and servants, husbands and wives, friends and relatives, life and death. But there are significant and surprising omissions. There is very little which is 'religious', no mention of priests and prophets, and very little about kings – all people who figure prominently in the rest of the Old Testament.

It is important that from the outset we are clear about the way in which we should view the subjects that are covered. Some people would make the mistake of claiming that Proverbs focuses upon 'secular' life, but the so-called 'secular/sacred divide' is not one that the Bible endorses. Indeed, as far as God is concerned, the only thing that can be described as 'secular' is sin itself.

The idea that only the 'religious' is 'sacred' comes from the Greek philosophers and has filtered into much modern thinking, even among Christians. The Bible knows of no such division. Any activity can be sacred if it can be devoted to God. He would rather have a good taxi driver than a bad missionary. All legitimate jobs are at the same level.

So Proverbs is interested in where most of our waking life is lived. This book tells us how we can make the most of life and warns us that many people waste it. It is about the 'Good Life'. Its wisdom enables us to arrive at the end of our days pleased with all that we have accomplished.

How is Proverbs related to the message of the rest of the Bible? The apostle Paul, in his second letter to Timothy, said that the holy Scriptures are able to make him 'wise for salvation through faith in Christ Jesus'. But a reading of Proverbs may leave us wondering where 'salvation' appears, since the themes of redemption that are common in other biblical books are strangely absent.

But the theme is there. The word 'salvation' is very close in meaning to words such as 'salvage' or 'recycling'. God is in the business of recycling people so that they become useful. Christians are changed from sinners into saints, but also from being *foolish* to being *wise*. The message of the Bible is that the real cause of pollution on the planet is people. Jesus himself likened hell to the rubbish dump in the valley of Gehenna outside Jerusalem, where all the garbage was thrown. He spoke of people being 'thrown' into hell as if they were good for nothing. God recycles people who are heading for hell, turning fools into wise people.

So in that sense Proverbs is full of 'salvation', since it tells us the sort of life we are saved for and reminds us about the sort of life we have been saved from. It thus corrects an imbalance that is common in the preaching of many churches. Too much attention is paid to what we are saved *from* and not enough to what we are saved *to* and *for*.

What about wisdom outside the Bible? Many would argue that there is a lot of wisdom that is not included in the Bible. What about the wisdom of Plato, Socrates, Aristotle and Confucius? It need not surprise us that there is wisdom outside the Bible, for all men and women are made in the image of God, and so they are able to make sense of life. But this is not to say that they have enough sense to make the *most* of life. Only when Christ redeems us do we grasp the real meaning of life and live as God intends. So in this respect the world's 'wisdom' will always be folly, for it lacks eternal perspective.

So Proverbs is affirming the truth that God is 'the All-Wise God', the source of all wisdom, and that it is his wisdom that created the whole universe, with all its complexity.

Why was Proverbs written?

Proverbs is unusual among the books of the Bible in that it tells us why it was written. The prologue says that learning from proverbs will lead us to wisdom, and it tells us that the very first step in becoming wise is to 'fear God' (that is, Yahweh, the God of the Jews). If we come to understand that he hates evil and that, as the all-seeing Judge, nothing escapes his attention, then we will see our poverty and our need for help in order to live life as he desires. Wisdom comes from fearing him, asking him for wisdom and learning how to handle the affairs of this world in a shrewd and sound way.

The book also tells us that wisdom comes from God via other people. God has chosen to pass on his wisdom especially through parents, grandparents and other people who are more experienced than us. So Proverbs contains many references to the family relationships that form the context in which wisdom is shared.

The author

The man who is most associated with wisdom in the Bible is the man who wrote the Book of Proverbs, King Solomon. On his accession to the throne God offered him anything he asked for, and he asked for wisdom to govern others. God gave him wisdom, along with other things that he didn't ask for, such as fame, power and wealth. His wise words were legendary, although he seemed to have more wisdom for others than for himself. After all, collecting 700 wives (and presumbably 700 mothers-in-law!) was hardly wise, not to mention 300 concubines.

But there was an important condition attached to God's promise of wisdom. He told Solomon in 1 Kings: 'I will give you a wise and discerning heart ... *if* you walk in my ways and obey my statutes and commands'. So we must conclude that the evident folly of his latter years was the result of neglecting these conditions.

In his prime, Solomon became so famous for his wisdom that the Queen of Sheba made a long journey not just to see his wealth but to hear his wisdom. Modern philosophers look back to the wise men of Greece such as Plato, Socrates and Aristotle, who lived around 400 years before Christ, but they forget that back in the Bronze Age, about 1,000 years before Christ, there was a wise man who was just as famous. Solomon wrote many of the proverbs in the Book of Proverbs, and he collected many others. He also wrote the Song of Songs and Ecclesiastes.

He wrote the Song of Songs when he was a young man, so much in love that he forgot about God altogether. It is a book of the heart. He wrote Proverbs when he was middle-aged. It is a book of the will. His last book, Ecclesiastes, was written in old age. It's a book of the mind, as he meditates on his life and wonders whether he has achieved anything with it. So we have

Solomon as a young lover, a middle-aged father and an elderly philosopher, writing these three books of wisdom.

One of the most intriguing things about the Book of Proverbs is that some of the proverbs in it come from outside Israel. There are some proverbs from Arabic philosophers, and a whole chapter from Egypt, probably collected through one of his wives, who was the daughter of Pharaoh. Solomon recognized that God had given wisdom to people outside the land of Israel, and so he was happy to include it in his work. These sayings were brought into the framework of a life lived under God.

But that is not to say that the Book of Proverbs does not have a strong reverence for God. God is mentioned 90 times in the book as *Yahweh*, the God of Israel – not some god that other nations might believe in. There is certainly no suggestion that the Arabic or Egyptian gods have any value.

Part of the collection was completed by King Hezekiah, who collected many of Solomon's unwritten proverbs some 250 years later, and these too are included in the book. So Proverbs as we have it today was not completed until about 550 BC.

The book's style

Before examining the content of the book, we need to consider some background points about its style and intention.

Proverbs, not promises

First, it is crucial to realize that this is a book of proverbs, not a book of promises. We should never quote a proverb as if it is a divine promise.

The English word 'proverb' comes from the Latin *proverba*. *Pro* means 'for' and *verba* means 'word'. The two combined mean 'a word for a situation'. A proverb is an appropriate word that fits the situation. It is thus a timeless truth that can be used in different situations in life.

The Hebrew word that we translate as 'proverb' is *maschal*, which means 'to resemble or to be like something'. Jesus began a number of parables with the phrase, 'The Kingdom of Heaven is like this ...'

So a proverb is a general observation on life, whereas a promise is a particular obligation.

Let me illustrate. Here is a proverb: 'Pawson has a passion for punctuality.' How is that proverb applied? It means that Pawson likes to be on time, but that is not the same as saying that Pawson makes a promise to be at a certain place by a certain time. I am not morally to blame if the proverb breaks down, but I am to blame if a promise breaks down. So a proverb is only *generally* true. We shouldn't apply a proverb to every situation and expect it to work. We must not assume that God is making promises to us when we read proverbs.

Thinking that a proverb is a promise has caused problems to many people. For example, 'honesty is the best policy'. This is generally true, but not always true. I know people who have lost a fortune through being honest!

Furthermore, proverbs can contradict each other – for example, 'more haste, less speed' and 'he who hesitates is lost'.

Turning to the Book of Proverbs, we find the same features. In chapter 26 we read, 'Do not answer a fool according to his folly', but the very next verse says, 'Answer a fool according to his folly'!

Two proverbs that have frequently been used as promises have caused Christians great consternation. One of them is 'Commit to the Lord whatever you do, and your plans will succeed'. Christians have started all sorts of business ventures on the basis of this verse. Although it is generally true, it doesn't

mean that every business venture that is committed to the
Lord is bound to be a success.

The second proverb that has caused problems is this:
'Train a child in the way he should go, and when he is old he
will not turn from it'.

Many parents with children who are not believers have a
problem with this verse. They say they trained their children
in the way they should go, but are disappointed that they seem
to have departed from it.

Once again, the proverb is not a promise – it is only generally true. Children are not puppets, and we can't force them to
go our way. They will reach an age when they will make their
own decision, and they are free to do so. Both these proverbs
are guidelines, not guarantees. If the users of the proverbs had
realized this, much heartache would have been averted.

Poetry

The second thing that we need to be aware of is that proverbs
are poetic. They are presented in a form that is easy to remember.

Let me translate a familiar proverb for you:

In advance of committing yourself to a course of action, consider carefully your circumstances and options.

Or, to rephrase:

There are certain corrective measures for minor problems
which, when taken early on in a course of action, forestall
major problems from arising.'

Those are both translations of 'Look before you leap'! Which
is easier to remember?!

We noted in Part I that Hebrew poetry is a unique form. It is not based on rhyme, as most English poetry is, but on rhythm. The rhythm is not only a matter of beat or metre; it is also a rhythm of thought. So Hebrew poetry often consists of pairs of lines (called parallelism) in which one line relates to the other in one of three different ways. In synonymous parallelism the thought in the first line is repeated in the second. For example:

Pride goes before destruction,
and a haughty spirit before a fall.

In *antithetical parallelism* the second line contrasts with the first one:

He who oppresses the poor shows contempt for their Maker,
but whoever is kind to the needy honours God.

In *synthetic parallelism* the thought in the first line is advanced by the second:

Stay away from a foolish man,
for you will not find knowledge on his lips.

In the examples above, the words *and*, *but* and *for* give a clue as to which type of parallelism is being used.

All the proverbs fit into this kind of pattern, but they are not as easy to remember in English because the rhythm is lost in translation. But Jewish parents passed on values to their children in this way, and we still do so today.

There are other devices that are used in Proverbs. Chapter 31 is arranged as an acrostic – that is, each line begins with a new letter of the Hebrew alphabet. On other occasions the structure is numerical: 'there are three things ... and four things ...' or 'there are six things God hates ...' and so on. These forms enable the reader/hearer to commit the proverb to memory.

Patriarchy

The third thing that we need to bear in mind is that this book is patriarchal. It is presented as a father's advice to a youth. It offers no advice at all to women! Such an approach is common throughout the Bible. For example, the letters in the New Testament are not addressed to 'brothers and sisters', but to 'brothers'. This apparent chauvinism is the result of one of the fundamental assumptions in Scripture – that is, that if the men are right, the women and the children will be right also. The Bible is deliberately addressed to men – precisely because it is their responsibility to lead their families, by teaching and example.

Wisdom and Folly

So in Proverbs we have Solomon, a middle-aged father, desperately trying to prevent a young man from committing the same errors as he did himself. He presents his son, and his readers, with the choice that they must make about how they will live their lives. Do they want Wisdom or Folly as their companion for life? He symbolically portrays both these options as women.

Wisdom personified

Chapters 8 and 9 describe Wisdom as a wonderful woman. The son is advised to love her like a sweetheart, to make her a beloved member of his family, to go after her, to court her. She says, 'I love those who love me, and those who seek me find me'.

Wisdom personalized

In chapter 31 (the acrostic chapter) a mother advises her son on what to look for in a good woman. She is to be a good wife, mother, neighbour and trader. Such a woman is vital to good, stable family life. She is 'more precious than rubies'.

Folly personified

The same pattern is used with Folly, which is personified in chapter 9. Folly seduces men with her smooth talk, enticing her prey with tempting offers. But for all who fall for her charms the end is death: 'She will destroy you, rob you of your manhood'.

Folly personalized

In chapter 6 Folly is depicted as a prostitute who reduces her victim to 'a loaf of bread'. To her he is no more than a meal ticket.

A biblical theme

This use of women as symbols is not unique to Proverbs. In the Book of Revelation there are two women – a filthy prostitute and a pure bride. The prostitute is called Babylon and the bride is called Jerusalem. So this theme runs through the whole Bible. Which woman is going to be your companion and your partner – folly or wisdom?

The Bible often presents us with choices, and this is the case in Proverbs. Will we choose life or death, light or darkness, heaven or hell?

Moral or mental?

Furthermore, Proverbs depicts wisdom and folly in another way: it tells us that they are *moral* choices rather than *mental* ones. When the world speaks of fools, it means people whose IQs aren't very high. But in the Bible someone who is very intelligent can be very foolish. Someone can be mentally clever and morally silly.

I once heard of a country yokel down in Somerset many years ago who had a strange reputation. If you offered him a sixpence or a £5 note, he always took the sixpence.

Thousands of tourists heard about this man and tried the trick on him. The poor, foolish man always took the coin, never the note. But really he was no fool – he made a fortune out of it!

Folly and wisdom have nothing to do with qualifications. In Psalm 14 the psalmist said, 'The fool says in his heart, "There is no God"'. The devil told Eve that eating the fruit would lead to wisdom, but in fact it only led to independence from God, the source of all wisdom. Worldly wisdom seeks to find the most profitable option, but biblical wisdom seeks what is best for your character. It is based not on knowledge of the world, but on knowledge of God.

This idea is backed up by a verse from chapter 29 that is often misunderstood: 'Where there is no vision the people perish' (AV). It is used when church leaders want to convince the congregation that their particular scheme should be followed. But in more modern translations the Hebrew word translated as 'vision' is more correctly translated as 'revelation', and the word 'perish' as 'cast off restraint' or 'become a fool'. So the verse is actually saying, 'If God isn't revealing things to you, you will become a fool.' So wisdom is practising God's presence in every area of life. We will need his Spirit's help if we are to understand his mind.

The book's structure

We turn now to consider the structure of the Book of Proverbs. The book has an amazing symmetry. Indeed, the only passage which doesn't really fit is the prologue at the beginning of the Arabic wisdom in chapter 30. Here is an outline of the book's structure:

PROLOGUE (1:1–7)
ADVICE TO YOUTH (1:8 – 9:18)
SOLOMON'S PROVERBS (10:1 – 22:16)
WISE WORDS (22:17 – 23:14)
ADVICE TO YOUTH (23:15 – 24:22)
WISE WORDS (24:23–34)
SOLOMON'S PROVERBS (25:1 – 29:27)
(AGUR [30:1–33])
ADVICE TO YOUTH (31:1–31)

It is arranged like a multi-layered sandwich. So 'Advice to Youth' provides the outer two layers, then the 'Proverbs of Solomon' are the next two layers, and then the 'Words of the Wise' sandwich 'Advice to Youth' in the middle.

Having seen the structure of the book, let us fill in some details:

PROLOGUE
Why the Proverbs were collected

ADVICE TO YOUTH (1:8 – 9:18)
From a father about bad women

1. *DO:*
   Obey your parents
   Seek and get wisdom
   Keep your heart
   Be faithful to your spouse

2. *DON'T:*
   Get into bad company
   Commit adultery
   Take out loans
   Be lazy
   Befriend foolish women

SOLOMON'S PROVERBS (**10:1 – 22:16**)
Collected by himself

1. *CONTRAST:* godly and wicked lives
2. *CONTENT:* godly life

WISE WORDS (**22:17 – 23:14**)
Egyptian (princess?)

ADVICE TO YOUTH (**23:15 – 24:22**)
More *DO's* ('get wise') and *DON'Ts* ('get drunk')

WISE WORDS (**24:23–34**)
Arab (numerical)

SOLOMON'S PROVERBS (**25:1 – 29:27**)
Copied by Hezekiah

1. *RELATIONSHIPS*
   with kings

neighbours
enemies
yourself
fools
sluggards
gossips

2. *RIGHTEOUSNESS* **(27:1 – 29:27)**
   humility in self
   justice for others
   fear of the Lord

ADVICE TO YOUTH (31:1–31)
From a mother about a good woman

1. *KING OF A NATION*
2. *QUEEN OF A HOME* **(31:10–31)**

The structure and content of the book make a number of things clear:

1 This is one of the few Bible books to spell out its purpose clearly – see the prologue.
2 These proverbs are especially pertinent for the royal family. There are 10 exhortations addressed to 'my son'. These are applicable especially to Solomon's own son, telling him the sort of company that he should keep and the sort of woman he should marry.
3 Most of the proverbs in chapters 10–15 use antithetic parallelism, whereas chapters 16–22 use synonymous parallelism.
4 Whilst we can discern a structure to the book as a whole, the proverbs themselves are not listed in a topical arrangement. They read like the advice that parents would give to a son

leaving home. They are disconnected and disorderly, but they cover the major areas. No parent would prearrange his or her advice into sections with a neat conclusion!

So for the purpose of analysis we will rearrange the proverbs and consider particular themes.

The wise man

In Proverbs a number of synonyms are used to describe wisdom: 'prudence', 'sensible', 'judicious', 'appropriate', 'careful to avoid undesirable consequences'. A wise man is contrasted with the fool, who is reckless, rash, careless and wasteful.

A wise man is able to discern between good and evil, and he knows how to respond to and deal with a situation. He is discreet and realistic, with power to make plans. He makes the most out of life.

The wise are open to correction and reproof, keen to turn away from their own independence and self-reliance towards the light of God's truth. Instead of fearing men, they fear God. The wise man values truth at any price, whether about himself, others or God.

The fool

There are over 70 proverbs about what a fool is like. A fool (always male) is described as ignorant, obstinate, arrogant, perverted, boring, aimless, inexperienced, irresponsible, gullible, careless, complacent, insolent, flippant, sullen, boorish, argumentative. He wants everything on a plate; he doesn't think for himself; he prefers fantasy to fact, illusions to truth. At best he is disturbing; at worst he is dangerous. He is a sorrow to his parents, yet he despises them as old-fashioned.

There are two particular fools in this fools' gallery. One is the *scoffer*, the debunker who is cynical and critical of everybody but himself. The other is the *sluggard*, the lazy man who is hinged to his bed. He is described as throwing his life down the drain.

Words

Another key subject in Proverbs is the tongue. Chapter 6 records seven abominations to the Lord: snobbery, lies, murder, conspiracy, mischief, perjury and gossip. The tongue figures in four of those. So sins of speech are a major topic throughout the book, for what is in the heart comes out of the mouth.

Words are powerful

Words cut deep. They can be cruel, clumsy and careless. Self-esteem can be ruined by words – they can make it too high or too low. Even bodily health can be affected. Our beliefs and convictions are formed by words. A timely word can have an enormous effect.

Words can spread like a prairie fire, causing strife, discord and division. They may be subtle hints, suggestions and innuendoes. But good words can reach many people as their benefit spreads across communities.

Words have their limits

Words are no substitute for deeds. The tongue can't alter facts. Brazen denial and the strongest excuses won't stand.

Words can't compel people to respond. Even the best teacher can't change an apathetic pupil, and even the worst gossip won't hurt the innocent. Only the malicious will pay any attention.

Healthy Speech

There are four categories of words that should be on our lips:

- Honest words – the straightforward 'yes' or 'no'.
- Few words – the less said, the better. Reticence to speak is a virtue.
- Calm words – words should be spoken from a cool spirit. A hot temper is rarely of benefit.
- Apt words – a word matched to the occasion, shaped for the benefit of the hearer or reader, can bring great joy.

Such speech needs time for reflection first. We need to know what we are talking about and to think through the implications before we speak.

Such speech also flows from a person's character, for what a person says comes from what they are. A person's words are worth what he or she is worth.

In the New Testament, James says that if anyone does not sin with his tongue, he is a perfect man.

Family

Proverbs is full of advice about relationships – both family relationships and friendships. The family unit is the pivot of society. Three of the ten commandments that God gave to Moses relate to the family, including the only commandment with a promise – 'Honour your father and your mother, so that you may live long in the land the Lord your God is giving you'. Proverbs holds before the reader the following ideals about the family:

Husband and wife: parents happily united

Proverbs teaches monogamy, despite the fact that it is written by Solomon! Parents should share their children's training and should speak with one voice. The man is to be loyal, but a woman can make or break her husband, bringing blessing or rottenness to his bones.

The book teaches a very high view of marriage and takes a serious view of any sin that would break a marriage up, especially sexual infidelity. A person who strays from the marriage bed loses honour and liberty, throws away their life, courts social disgrace and physical danger. In short, they commit moral suicide.

Parents and children: children faithfully trained

We are told that parents are fools if they don't discipline their children. 'Spare the rod and spoil the child' is one of the better-known proverbs. The book also says that discipline is a loving act. There is no suggestion that this is a cure-all for parents. We also learn that foolishness is bound up in the heart of a child. They are free to welcome or despise the instruction they are given. Proverbs teaches that children are naturally foolish and need encouragement to be wise. This is diametrically opposed to today's humanistic philosophy that says that the child is basically good and will turn out well if given the right environment. The Bible is so blunt as to say that if you don't punish your children quickly when they are doing wrong, you don't love them.

There is teaching on the need to train children in righteousness from an early age, seeking to foster wise habits, so that they think and act in ways that will bring joy and pride and not shame and disgrace. Even the best teaching cannot force obedience; it can only encourage wise choices. Even sons of the best parents may still be too rebellious, lazy, indulgent or proud to take advice. They can use up a family fortune and neglect a greedy parent in old age.

Brothers (including cousins and other relatives)

Not many of the proverbs are directly concerned with the horizontal relationships in the family. The book describes the kind of relationship where the brother is helpful and faithful, and also the kind which brings discord, injury and bitterness.

Friendships

The Hebrew word that is translated 'friend' also means 'neighbour'. It refers to all non-relatives who live within the immediate circle of one's relationships. The advice of the book contrasts with today's depersonalized world where true friendship is rare.

Good neighbours

Good neighbours promote peace and harmony, are reluctant to quarrel and are disarmingly kind. They are generous in their judgements and always willing to give help when needed. They appreciate the importance of silence and privacy. They say 'No' to unwise agreements.

Good friends

Proverbs teaches that a few good friends is better than a host of acquaintances. A good friend can be closer than a relative.

A good friend has four qualities:

- *Loyalty* – will stick with you, no matter what.
- *Honesty* – will be frank with you and tell you the truth.
- *Consultancy* – will give you advice. An opposite viewpoint may be what is required.
- *Courtesy* – will always respect your feelings and refuse to trade on your affection.

Conclusion

What should we make of the Book of Proverbs? Let us begin by asking whether it achieved its objective. Israel was now in a position of peace and prosperity. Solomon realized that they could lose all this so easily (although he didn't realize that he himself would cause that loss).

In chapter 14 we are told that 'Righteousness exalts a nation, but sin is a disgrace to any people'. Solomon collected the proverbs into a book because he knew that without wisdom it would be impossible for Israel to remain in peace and prosperity. But Israel largely ignored the wisdom they received; they moved further away from God. Indeed, even Solomon didn't live by his own wisdom.

There is a great deal in the New Testament that builds on the Book of Proverbs and focuses on the theme of wisdom. The book is quoted 14 times directly, and there are many other occasions when it is alluded to.

In Luke 1 we read that John the Baptist came 'to turn … the disobedient to the wisdom of the righteous'. Jesus spoke with such wisdom that his hearers asked where he got this wisdom from.

Most people are familiar with the Wise Men who followed a star to Bethlehem. Whilst they have been commonly regarded as Gentiles, it is more likely that they were descendants of the Jews who had been left behind in Babylon after the Exile. They had remembered the prophecy of Balaam, that a star would arise out of Israel to be the King of the Nations (Numbers 24), so when they saw it they followed it. Their presence in Matthew's birth narrative says much about the importance of Christ's incarnation.

Jesus was said to be 'filled with wisdom' as a child (Luke 2). In his public ministry he said that the Queen of Sheba came from the ends of the earth to listen to Solomon's wisdom, but now One greater than Solomon had come (Luke 11). When Jesus was criticized for eating and drinking, he replied that 'wisdom is proved right by all her children' (Luke 7).

Reflecting on the life of Jesus, the apostle Paul wrote in 1 Corinthians 1 that 'Christ is our wisdom. He has become for us wisdom from God'.

The wisdom of God is seen supremely in the cross. The world says that dying on a cross is sheer folly. But Paul says that what was foolishness to the world was the wisdom of God.

Within the New Testament epistles there are many direct quotations from the Book of Proverbs. Paul writes in Romans 12: 'If your enemy is hungry, feed him; if he is thirsty, give him something to drink. In doing this, you will heap burning coals on his head'.

Peter frequently quotes from Proverbs. For example, in 2 Peter 2 he quotes from Proverbs 26: 'As a dog returns to its vomit, so a fool repeats his folly.' Peter's exhortation to his readers to 'fear the Lord and honour the King' comes straight out of Proverbs 24.

In Hebrews 12 the writer quotes from Proverbs 3 with respect to God's discipline of his children: 'My son, do not make light of the Lord's discipline, and do not lose heart when he rebukes you, because the Lord disciplines those he loves, and he punishes everyone he accepts as a son'.

In Proverbs 30, Agur asks the question, 'Who has gone up to heaven and come down?' Jesus answers this very question in John 3, when he speaks of his own journey from heaven to earth.

But the Letter of James is where the Proverbs are especially used. This epistle has been called the New Testament version of Proverbs, since it is so similar in style. It moves swiftly from topic to topic with little sense of order, just like its Old Testament counterpart. Some of the themes in James come from Proverbs, not least a devastating analysis of the evils of the tongue and a description of the benefits of wisdom.

Proverbs may seem a strange book to be included in the Bible, but closer inspection shows that its place is thoroughly justified. It deals with some of the major themes of Scripture, it is quoted and alluded to by other parts of the Bible and is an important part of the Christian's arsenal in his or her fight against foolish living. But it is not an easy book. Care must be taken in reading it, and many of its lessons will find us out.

PART IV

ECCLESIASTES

Introduction

The Book of Ecclesiastes includes some statements that many would regard as debatable. Consider which of the following you would agree with:

■ Generations come and generations go, but the world stays just the same.
■ A man is no better off than an animal, because life has no meaning for either.
■ It is better to be satisfied with what you have than to always want something else.
■ A working man may or may not have enough to eat, but at least he can get a good night's sleep. A rich man has so much that he stays awake worrying!
■ Don't be too good or too wise. Why kill yourself? But don't be too wicked or too foolish either. Why die before you have to?
■ I found one man in a thousand that I could respect, but not one woman!
■ Fast runners do not always win the race, and the brave do not always win the battle.
■ Put your investment in several places – in many places, even – because you never know what kind of bad luck you're going to have in this world!

There's a saying which is especially true for our study of this book: 'A text out of context becomes a pretext.' In other words, we must see how the text functions within the book in which it is found before we quote it. The above statements were part of the writer's reflections, but they must not be taken out of the context of the book as a whole.

Ecclesiastes is probably the strangest book in the Bible. Although it is easy to understand, it says the most outrageous things. In places it reads like the mottoes on slips of paper that we find in Christmas crackers. In other places it has a poetic quality. These lines from the English poet, Alfred Lord Tennyson, could easily have been written by the author of Ecclesiastes:

> 'Tis better to have loved and lost
> Than never to have loved at all.
>
> *In Memoriam*

> For men at most differ as heaven and earth,
> But women, worst and best, as heaven and hell.
>
> *Pelleas and Ettare*

> Authority forgets a dying king.
>
> *Morte' d'Arthur*

> Our little systems have their day,
> They have their day and cease to be.
>
> *In the Valley of Cauteretz*

> Because right is right, to follow right
> Were wisdom in the scorn of consequence.
>
> *The Revenge*

But despite its strangeness, Ecclesiastes has a very contemporary ring to it and features many of the philosophical ideas of our own day:

- *Fatalism:* whatever will be, will be.
- *Existentialism:* live for the present moment – who knows what the future will bring?
- *Chauvinism:* men are better than women.
- *Hedonism:* living for pleasure.
- *Cynicism:* even good things aren't what they seem.
- *Pessimism:* things are bound to get worse.

The book's author

This book of philosophical speculation comes from King Solomon, who has reached the end of his life and is disappointed, disillusioned and hopeless. When we read Solomon's three books, it is easy to tell how old he was when he wrote them. The Song of Songs was written when he was a young man, deeply in love. Proverbs is the book of a middle-aged man trying to stop his son from falling into the same errors that he himself succumbed to. But in Ecclesiastes we have the writings of an older man. Confirmation of this is found in a verse towards the end of the book, in chapter 12: 'Remember your Creator in the days of your youth, before the days of trouble come and the years approach when you will say, "I find no pleasure in them"'.

As an old man, he has reflected deeply upon life. He is fond of the phrase, 'I saw …' The insights in this book are the result of his observations.

The book's style

Solomon gives himself the Hebrew title *Qohelet*, a word that is translated in various ways: 'preacher', or 'philosopher' or 'lecturer'. But the best translation is 'speaker', particularly as this is also the title of the person who presides over the debates in the House of Commons, and so conveys very well the way in which the book is written. For it is written in the style of an old man presiding over a debate – a debate that is going on in his mind. Like every good speaker, he allows the pros and the cons to be given equal opportunity. So the motion that life is not worth living is followed by a motion proclaiming that it is.

As such, the book is contemporary for all centuries, as people have always engaged in similar debates, especially as they reach their forties and ask, 'What is it all about?' Some people make radical changes in their lifestyle because they feel that they are missing out on life.

In Ecclesiastes, Solomon is asking some big questions. What is life about? Is life worth living? How can we make the most of life? He is asking the right questions, even if he hasn't found the right answers. His concerns and answers oscillate throughout the book. His *message* is sometimes optimistic, sometimes pessimistic. His *mood* is at one time uplifting, then depressing. The book's *merit* switches from the profound to the superficial and back again.

Negative statements

Solomon's opening statement is a profoundly negative one: 'Meaningless! Meaningless! ... Everything is meaningless!'. The word translated as 'meaningless' could also be rendered as 'emptiness'. Here's a man who gets to the end of his life and says that it's all been pointless and useless.

It is important to remember that Solomon was a king who had the power to do anything he wanted and the wealth to indulge every whim. The book mentions the huge range of activities in which Solomon engaged in an attempt to find the happiness that eluded him.

He tried science and agriculture, even breeding his own cattle. Then he moved on to the arts. No doubt he inherited a love of music from his father. He built some great buildings. He gathered pictures from around the world and placed them in a gallery. Then he turned to entertainment, with court comedians visiting him in his palace. But none of this satisfied him. He was involved in business, and amassed a fortune in the commercial world. He tried pleasure – food, wine and women. Still dissatisfied, he turned to philosophy and bought many books, including some from Egypt. They stimulated him but failed to meet his deepest needs.

There was nothing wrong with these interests in themselves, but they failed to provide what he was looking for. His life was filled but not fulfilled, and at times he wished that he was just an ordinary man.

We can explain his failure to make sense of life. The nub of his problem was that he has *observed* so much but had *perceived* so little. He had tunnel vision – he was looking at life through one eye, as in a telescope, but he had no depth and no perspective.

There were two limitations in particular:

1. Space

On 28 occasions he uses a phrase to describe the location of everything he saw: it was 'under the sun', a phrase that occurs nowhere else in the whole Bible. If our vision is limited to this earth and this life, we will never understand what life is all about and what makes it worth living. We will have to depend upon finding fulfilment in the fleeting pleasures that the world can offer.

2. Time

Solomon also uses the phrase 'while we are still alive'. He assumes that death is the end of meaningful, conscious existence. He has no thought of the afterlife, which can give perspective and meaning to the years of life that we are allotted.

Our modern age shares some of Solomon's tunnel vision. It often observes the world in scientific terms that assume that there is no God and no life to come. Science can tell us how the world came into being, but not why. Solomon needs to look at life from a different angle, but this will only come if he looks at it from God's viewpoint.

Positive statements

The unresolved questions of the book sometimes give way to optimism. Our ignorance need not lead to despair; it may be that we are ignorant because no one knows, or because God knows but we don't yet see it ourselves. Whenever Solomon brings God into his thinking, he becomes more positive. There are two passages in Ecclesiastes where this is especially true.

The first is in chapter 3. This is the best known and most frequently quoted section of the book. Its verses have often been used as titles for novels and films. It is a poem with a lovely rhythm, reminding us that there is a time and place for everything.

God is sovereign,
Sets the seasons:
Date of birthday,
Day of death.
Time for planting,
Time for reaping;
Time for killing,
Time to heal.

Time for wrecking,
Time for building;
Time for sorrow,
Time for joy.
Time for mourning,
Time for dancing;
Time for kissing,
Time to stop!

Time for finding,
Time for losing;
Time for saving,
Time for waste.
Time for tearing,
Time for mending;
Time for silence,
Time to talk.

Time for loving,
Time for hating;
Time for fighting,
Time for peace.
Have your fun, then,
But remember ...

God is sovereign;
HE decrees.[1]

Most readers miss a key verse when the poetry ends and the text returns to prose. We read that God himself 'has made everything beautiful in its time'. So the overall emphasis is not upon human decision but divine decree. The New English Bible translates the verse as follows: 'Everything that happens in this world happens at the time God chooses.'

It is this perspective that brings light to our pessimism about life. When we believe that our lives are in God's hands and that he knows the right time for us to dance and to weep, then we see that the things that happen to us are not chance, but part of God's choice for us. He is weaving a pattern out of our lives.

Some believe that this approach is fatalistic, that it suggests an impersonal fate that nobody can affect. But this is quite different from God freely choosing what he allows to happen to us. Our free will never overrides God's. He will be at work in all things to achieve his purposes. He calls us to choose his way, surrendering our wills to his sovereign control. We are both accountable and responsible for the lives we live.

This approach to life is reflected elsewhere in the Bible. We are encouraged to see all the plans we make in the light of God's sovereign will. All plans are made 'God willing'. My father had a favourite saying: 'Life is long enough to live out God's purpose, but it's too short to waste a moment.' This is the message of chapter 3. Our times are in his hands, and he will decide what is best for us in the future.

The other passage that has a strong sense of the presence of God is in chapters 11 and 12. The Living Bible translates it as follows:

1 This may be sung to the popular tune, 'I am sailing'.

It is a wonderful thing to be alive! If a person lives to be very old, let him rejoice in every day of life, but let him also remember that eternity is far longer, and that everything down here is futile in comparison.

Young man, it's wonderful to be young! Enjoy every minute of it! Do all you want to; take in everything, but realize that you must account to God for everything you do.

So banish grief and pain, but remember that youth, with a whole life before it, can make serious mistakes.

Don't let the excitement of being young cause you to forget about your Creator.

Honour him in your youth before the evil years come – when you'll no longer enjoy living. It will be too late then to try to remember him, when the sun and light and moon and stars are dim to your old eyes, and there is no silver lining left among your clouds. For there will come a time when your limbs will tremble with age, and your strong legs will become weak, and your teeth will be too few to do their work, and there will be blindness, too. Then let your lips be tightly closed while eating, when your teeth are gone! And you will waken at dawn with the first note of the birds; but you yourself will be deaf and tuneless, with quavering voice. You will be afraid of heights and of falling – a white-haired, withered old man, dragging himself along: without sexual desire, standing at death's door, and nearing his everlasting home as the mourners go along the streets.

Yes, remember your Creator now while you are young, before the silver cord of life snaps, and the golden bowl is broken, and the pitcher is broken at the fountain, and the wheel is broken at the cistern; and the dust returns to the earth as it was, and the spirit returns to God who gave it. All is futile, says the Preacher; utterly futile.

But then, because the Preacher was wise, he went on teaching the people all he knew; and he collected proverbs and classified them. For the Preacher was not only a wise man, but a good teacher; he not only taught what he knew to the people, but taught them in an interesting manner.

The wise man's words are like goads that spur to action. They nail down important truths. Students are wise who master what their teachers tell them.

But, my son, be warned: there is no end of opinions ready to be expressed. Studying them can go on forever, and become very exhausting!

Here is my final conclusion: fear God and obey his commandments, for this is the entire duty of man. For God will judge us for everything we do, including every hidden thing, good or bad.

There are some helpful points to note in this last passage of the book:

Remember

Solomon urges his hearers, especially those who are young, to remember God. This advice probably came from his own experience – the Song of Songs has no mention of God, for example. He is saying that he would not have faced the trauma of wondering what life was all about if he had only remembered God earlier in his life.

Fear

He urges his hearers to fear God. The wisdom literature of the Bible constantly tells us that the fear of the Lord is the beginning of wisdom. If we truly fear God, we are not afraid of anything or anyone else. We must fear God, because he is going to ask us for an account of the life he has given us.

Jesus told his followers not to fear those who can kill the body but rather to 'Fear him who, after the killing of the body, has power to throw you into hell' (Luke 12). If people outside the Church don't fear God, it's because people inside it don't fear him either.

Obey

Solomon knew that he had not obeyed God as he should. Nevertheless he tells his readers to be careful to obey God. He now knows that God's laws are given for our good, not to spoil life but to help us to make the most of it. He talks of this as 'the whole duty of man' (chapter 12). Our responsibilities are more important than our rights.

Conclusion

Solomon had collected and collated proverbs, but he had delved into too many other philosophies as well. Here was a man who had read too much and had become disillusioned in the process. So much of the emptiness in the Book of Ecclesiastes comes from these other philosophies. The book shows the limits of human wisdom and is a salutary reminder of the sort of person we will become if we don't discover God's way to live.

God has included this strange book in the Bible because it allows us to examine the wrong ideas alongside the good and true ones. It faces us with the pessimistic and fatalistic view of life, showing us the best that human thinking can provide.

It tells us that if we don't understand the meaning of life from heaven's angle and from the angle of the next world, we finish up disillusioned, disappointed and depressed.

Of course, the Bible doesn't leave us with the pessimism of this book. The New Testament tells us that Christ is our wisdom. Through him we find out both *why* and *how* we should live life.

John 17 tells us that true life is to know him. He is the Alpha and the Omega, the One who ensures that life really does have meaning and purpose.

PART V

JOB

Introduction

Many common phrases in the English language come from the Book of Job. Someone who shows fortitude in the face of great suffering is said to have 'the patience of Job'. People whose words make the sufferer feel worse are called 'Job's comforters'.

The Anglican funeral service uses a line from the early part of the book: 'the Lord gave, and the Lord hath taken away; blessed be the name of the Lord' (AV). Music lovers will be familiar with the refrain, 'I know that my redeemer liveth' (AV), which Handel used in the *Messiah*. But despite people's familiarity with a few verses from Job, the book as a whole is not well known. Most people fail to understand the purpose of the book, and are thus unable to put the parts that they do know into an appropriate context.

The Book of Job may be one of the oldest books that we possess today, though it is not easy to date it. We know that it comes from Abraham's era, because so many details in the book could only fit that period. The author uses the name 'Yahweh' to refer to God, just as Moses does, but there is no trace of the Exodus, the Covenant of Sinai or the Law of Moses, which were so fundamental to the Old Testament.

Readers of Job are immediately faced with a question that determines the way in which they read the book. Is it fact, fiction or a mixture of the two – 'faction'?

Fact?

Those who believe it to be fact emphasize that other biblical writers treat Job as a real person. Ezekiel lists him with Noah and Daniel as one of the three most righteous men who ever lived. In the New Testament, James refers to Job's perseverance as an example for his readers.

Furthermore, the opening chapter tells us that Job lived 'In the land of Uz'. Although the whereabouts of Uz is uncertain, we can be confident that Job lived in the Mesopotamian Basin, around the Rivers Tigris and Euphrates beyond Damascus.

In addition, the story line suggests a real person. His reactions to the disasters that he faces are realistic and the descriptions of his personal feelings seem authentic. His discussions with his wife are what we might typically expect, and the comments of his friends and the arguments that follow seem true to life. His ownership of significant numbers of livestock is normal for a wealthy farmer.

Fiction?

Many are unconvinced by these arguments. Despite the plausibility of so much of the book, the reader has a sense that there is something that doesn't seem to ring true to life.

For example, take the events of the first chapter. There are four consecutive disasters, with each leaving one survivor who returns to Job to describe the incident. It is stretching credulity to think that all four disasters have just one survivor and that each would choose the same words: 'I am the only one who has escaped to tell you!'

Also the happy ending seems contrived. Job loses all his children in the first scene, yet in the last he has exactly the same number of new children – seven boys and three girls. We are clearly supposed to rejoice in the happy ending, almost as if the loss of his former children is insignificant to him. It makes us ask the question, 'Is this too neat for reality? Are we supposed to take this as fact?'

Questions about the factual basis of the book are also raised when we consider the speeches, for each one is written in Hebrew poetry. We have already noted in Part I that poetry is an artificial form of speech. It would not be used in conversation, and certainly not to discuss the weighty issues considered by Job and his friends. Yet all Job's 'comforters' speak in superbly crafted poems, which begs the question, 'Who committed the poetry to paper?' Either all his friends were brilliant poets with outstanding memories, or we will have to think of an alternative explanation.

'Faction'?

The only solution that makes sense is to say that the Book of Job is *faction* – that is, it is based on fact, but the facts have been enlarged and embroidered. So Job is a real person who has to make sense of disaster and ongoing suffering, alongside a belief in the God of the Bible.

So the Book of Job is similar to some of the plays of William Shakespeare, who took the basic historical facts about people such as Henry V and produced plays that emphasized the inner motivations of the characters. A more modern example would be Robert Bolt's play, *A Man for All Seasons*, based on the life of Sir Thomas More. Bolt captures the essence of the issues that the man faced, but the audience knows that the end product is not the same as the real events.

Literature

The Book of Job is written in Hebrew poetry that depends upon sense and repetition and not upon sound for its beauty. It is a great work of literature and defies strict classification. It combines epic poetry, drama and debate with an intriguing plot and profound dialogue. Not surprisingly, the book has been much admired by some of the greatest minds. Thomas Carlyle said, 'It is a noble book', Alfred Lord Tennyson described it as 'the greatest poem of ancient or modern times' and Martin Luther said, 'It is most magnificent, sublime, as no other book of Scripture.' It has been placed on a par with the works of Homer, Virgil, Dante, Milton and Shakespeare as one of the greatest pieces of literature of all time.

Philosophy

But Job is more than a great work of literature – it is also a work of philosophy. It asks the questions that philosophers have pondered throughout the history of mankind: Why are we here? What is life about? Where did evil come from? Why do good people suffer? What is God's involvement in the world? Is he interested and does he care?

Job covers all these themes, but especially the question, Why do good people suffer? Job was clearly a good man, but experienced the most appalling tragedy. The book addresses the issue of why this should be.

Theology

Job is also a book of theology. Philosophy can deal with the big questions in an abstract manner, but theology relates these questions to God. It is important to note from the outset that only those who have a particular view of God have difficulties with the fact of suffering. If you believe that God is bad, then there is no problem about suffering, because you would expect a bad God to make you suffer. Only if you believe that God is good do you have a problem. Furthermore, you may believe that God is good but weak, and so is unable to do anything to help you. Again, on the grounds of logic, you should then have no problem with suffering, since a weak God can sympathize but cannot help. Only when we believe that God is both *able* to help and *good* in his nature do we have a problem with suffering.

Many 'modern theologians' try to avoid the problem of suffering by denying one or the other of those two things: they reason that either God is bad and is playing tricks on us, or he is too weak to affect anything. But it is clear that the author of the Book of Job believes:

1 that there is one God.
2 that he relates to his creatures.
3 that he is the almighty, all-powerful Creator.
4 that he is good, caring and compassionate.

Yet at the same time the book describes Job's situation, which seems to fly in the face of such beliefs. The reader is left to see how Job deals with this conflict and how God makes himself known in the midst of it.

Wisdom literature

It is important that we also understand that the Book of Job is part of the 'wisdom literature' in English Bibles, along with Proverbs, Psalms, Ecclesiastes and the Song of Songs. In the Hebrew Bible these books are called the 'Writings', a miscellaneous collection of texts which came out of the prophetic period but which are not regarded as prophecy. Understanding the Book of Job in this way should help us to interpret it correctly, because some statements in wisdom literature can be misleading. Let me explain in more detail.

First, not everything in wisdom literature is right. It includes passages where men wrestle with questions. Their statements do not always reflect God's mind, but they are included to show the argument being made, and providing that we see their purpose, we can interpret them without any problem. Job's friends make many statements based on a limited understanding. They are given to show us examples of how people come to terms with suffering, but to take any of their statements out of context, as if they expressed God's mind on the matter, would be the height of folly. Every statement in the Bible must be seen in the context of the book in which it appears. The message of the book as a whole determines the meaning of any statement within it.

Secondly, it is important to note that wisdom literature is general and not particular. This means that words of wisdom are not always true in every situation. The Book of Proverbs, for example, is not a list of promises but includes sayings that are generally true most of the time.

If you try to claim that they are true in every situation, you will be disappointed. This gives the clue to the problem that Job and his friends faced. They were aware of proverbs indicating that if you live a bad life you suffer for it. This is often true, but not always, and Job is part of the 'but not always'. The Book of Job is trying to deal with the exceptions to the rule.

A Jewish perspective

We must bear in mind one acute difference between a Jewish understanding of this book and a Christian one. The Jew of Old Testament times was unable to see the problems of temporal life in the light of eternity. He felt that the justice of God must be seen in this life, since both good and bad people went to the same destination – *Sheol*, the place of shadowy existence where departed spirits slept.

Christians, of course, have a totally different perspective on present suffering. In the light of Christ's work, they see the bigger picture of heaven. Suffering in this world is small compared to the life that will be enjoyed in heaven.

So throughout the Book of Job there are only hints about life after death. Job declares at one point that he will see God when he is dead, but this is not a common theme, and he certainly does not understand how this might take place.

The book's structure

The introduction creates a marvellous tension that underpins the whole framework of the book. God makes a wager with Satan, and that wager is settled in Job's body. But at no point does Job know that the wager has taken place. So this secret, known by the reader, helps to keep us guessing as Job faces the dilemmas of his situation.

Such a plot is extremely risky, as it makes suggestions about God's character and activity, in particular, his relationship with

Satan, which would be the height of blasphemy if it were not true – that God himself was responsible for Satan's attack on this good man.

Let us now consider how the book is structured:

THE PROLOGUE (chapters 1–2) (prose)
Two rounds: God versus Satan.

THE DIALOGUE (3:1–42:6) (poetry)
1. *Human* (3–37)
   (a) Eliphaz, Bildad, Zophar (3–31)
       (i)   Round One (3–14)
       (ii) Round Two (15–21)
       (iii) Round Three (22–31)
   (b) Elihu (32–37) – a monologue

2. *Divine* (38:1–42:6)
       (i) Round One (38–39)
       (ii) Round Two (40:1–42:6)

THE EPILOGUE (42:7–17) (prose)
Final rounds: God versus Job.

The Book of Job is arranged like a sandwich. The prose is the 'bread', providing the story and the background at the beginning and the end, while the poetry is the 'filling' in the middle, consisting of the debate that Job has with his three friends and a youth who appears when the friends have left.

The epilogue provides the resolution to what has gone before. It is a happy ending, with a difference.

Two plots

There are two plots skilfully woven together – a heavenly plot
and an earthly plot. The events that happen on earth are the
result of something that has already happened in heaven – just
as in the Book of Revelation there is war on earth directly after
a war in heaven.

The divine plot

The book begins with the heavenly plot – God's meeting in
heaven with Satan. Satan was an angel whose job was to report
sins. He was God's counsel for the prosecution who travelled
across the earth to report to God what human beings were like.
By the time of Job, Satan had reached such a point of cynicism
that he couldn't believe that anyone would love God for his
own sake. He thought people only loved God for what they
could get out of him.

So there is a debate between God and Satan, with Satan
arguing this very point. God asks Satan whether he met Job
when he visited the earth. God argues that Job loves him because
he loves him, and not because of any blessing he has received.

Satan continues to be cynical in his reply, claiming that if
God were to take away his blessings, Job would curse God just
like all the others. And so the heavenly wager takes place.

The key to every good drama is tension. While the reader
is aware of the heavenly wager, Job is not. If he knew, the test
would not be valid.

This interaction teaches us important lessons about Satan.
First, it implies that he cannot be in more than one place at
once. He does not have God's omnipresence. So when people
say that Satan is troubling them because something trivial has
gone wrong, they are mistaken. He generally has more important work to do with other people! What some people call

'satanic attack' should be more properly called 'demonic attack'. Satan's forces are at work all over the world, but that is not to say that Satan himself is personally involved.

This wrong thinking about Satan has arisen partly because we follow the error of the ancient Greeks and divide the world into the 'natural' and the 'supernatural'. We assume that Satan must be supernatural, and so we place him alongside God, as if he is equal in power and authority. Instead we should divide the world as the Bible does, with the Creator on one side and his creatures (including Satan) on the other. Satan is not omnipotent, omniscient or omnipresent; he is a mere creature.

Secondly, Satan needs God's permission to attack Job. Satan cannot touch a person who belongs to God unless God gives him permission. In the New Testament, God promises all believers that they will never be tempted above what they can bear, because he controls the tempter.

The human plot

The larger part of the book describes the debate between Job and his friends. The key question that is addressed is, 'Why is Job suffering more than other people?'

There are two viewpoints:

a   the friends are sure that the suffering has come because Job is sinning;
b   Job is quite sure that he's not sinning and protests his innocence.

Since the reader knows that Job is correct, the dialogue is alive with tension.

The two-plot structure of the book reminds us that none of us knows the whole picture when it comes to understanding the reason for suffering. Beyond looking for reasons, everyone is faced with a bigger question: Can I continue to believe in a good God when everything's going wrong? The Book of Job gives an answer to this question.

The importance of this issue is clarified by asking, 'What was Job's greatest pain?' Was it

■ *physical?* He was afflicted with sores from head to toe, he was tired and weary, and was in considerable physical pain.
■ *social?* His physical appearance and the local community's knowledge of his recent tragedy made him a social outcast. He sat on the ash-heap at the end of the village, and people walked on the other side of the street rather than talk to him. Even the teenagers laughed at him.
■ *mental?* He faced the mental pain of not knowing why these distressing things were happening to him, especially as there seemed to be nothing in his past to point to.
■ *spiritual?* His spiritual pain was far greater than any other, for he felt that he had lost touch with God. He cried out, asking that he might find him, talk to him, even argue with him! This was the real, the deepest pain. The agony of suffering is compounded if we feel that God is far away and no longer cares. (However, when Job was finally able to speak with God, it didn't turn out as he had imagined.)

The prologue

The prologue introduces us to the characters in the story:

God

God (who is called *Yahweh*) initiates the whole series of events by challenging Satan.

Satan

Satan is the counsel for the prosecution. In the Hebrew text he is called '*the* satan', which means 'the accuser'; 'satan' is not yet a proper name.

Job

Job is described as 'blameless and upright; he feared God and shunned evil'. Those two things belong together: the fear of God leads to the shunning of evil. If you lack the fear of God, then you're not so worried about sin. God is clearly pleased with Job's piety and has blessed him with children, property and good health.

Job's wife

It is difficult to write about Job's wife without appearing negative! The text describes her as 'a foolish woman', meaning that she is insensitive to Job's plight. She urges him to 'Curse God and die!'. Just when he needs support and help, she is the first one to bring him pain. She tells Job that God has deserted him and proceeds to do the same.

Job's friends

Job's three friends are older than him. They begin by sitting with him and not saying a word for seven days.

The human dialogue

Job eventually breaks the silence by cursing the day he was born. He wishes he had been stillborn and had gone to *Sheol*, which was the unconscious, shadowy afterlife that the people of Old Testament times believed in. At least then he would be at peace instead of in constant pain. It is gloomy, self-pitying talk, though never for one moment does he think of taking his life.

Each of the three friends speaks three times, but for the purposes of analysis we will put their speeches together.

Eliphaz

Eliphaz's speeches suggest that he is an elder statesman – a pious, mystical man. Unlike Job's other friends, he is gentle in his approach. He believes that Job is being punished because he has sinned. He bases his view on the orthodox doctrine of reward and punishment, on history itself, and on the cumulative wisdom of the age. In short, if Job has not sinned, then why is he being punished?

Furthermore, he makes reference to a vision he has had, which has confirmed to him that Job's punishment is thoroughly merited by his behaviour. He explains that because human nature is inherently evil, nobody can say that they are innocent before God. Since we are all sinners, Job should just admit that sin is the reason for his pain. When Job asks why he suffers more than others, Eliphaz tells him that suffering is God's way of making him a better person.

Although the advice is very gentle, Job doesn't take it, so Eliphaz becomes more impassioned in his argument, claiming that Job is obstinate to insist on his innocence, and also that he is irreverent and keen to undermine religious belief. Eliphaz clearly resents Job's antipathy to his views, and eventually his sympathy gives way to sarcasm. He argues that since we are all totally depraved, we can't grumble about suffering. The wicked won't prosper, and even if they do, they won't be happy – they will only seem to be happy.

Finally, when Job still doesn't respond, Eliphaz speaks of God's transcendence. He claims that God is too big to be concerned, so Job shouldn't expect God's attention.

A transcendent God can't be bothered with every individual life.

Bildad

Bildad's name actually means 'God's darling', but his words fail to match his name. Traditionally, the older person would speak first in such a situation, and Bildad is clearly a bit younger than Eliphaz – probably around 50 years of age.

Bildad is the 'theologian' of the three and a traditionalist *par excellence*. He is full of clichés, jargon and formulas, and has very little patience or compassion for Job. He tells Job that he has lost his children because they were sinners who deserved God's wrath. He believes in a moral universe, with the law of cause and effect applying to our moral life as well as to our material life.

As far as Bildad is concerned, if you sin, you suffer, so Job must be a pretty bad sinner. It is not surprising that in the course of the dialogue his relationship with Job becomes increasingly strained.

Eventually he tells Job that he is talking nonsense. He takes refuge in God's omnipotence, asking Job if he has forgotten that God is all-powerful. Since God is bigger than we are, we can't argue with him, so why not just accept it?

His bottom line is similar to the argument that Eliphaz made: God's omnipotence is the answer.

Zophar

The next man to speak with Job is the most dogmatic of the three. He is younger than the first two, but still middle-aged. We might call Zophar 'Joe Blunt', because he accuses Job of talking to cover up his guilt. He claims that even if Job isn't consciously sinning, he must be sinning unconsciously. He insults Job and tells him to choose between the broad way and the narrow way – that is, the wicked way and the righteous way. He admits to being puzzled by the prosperity of the wicked, but claims that it is short-lived. Since Job's prosperity has gone, he must be wicked. Zophar reminds Job that God is omniscient, and so he knows the sins that Job is not conscious of.

***

The arguments of Job's three 'friends' have much in common. They all assume that we live in a cause-and-effect moral universe, and they try to force the facts to fit their beliefs. They take refuge in doctrine and they try to force it upon Job insensitively. Indeed, their arguments are examples of how *not* to apply biblical doctrine! We need to hold firmly to clear doctrines, but we also need to be careful about how we apply them to individual cases. For example, it is sometimes true to say that someone is not healed because they don't have faith, but one would need considerable wisdom to know when this maxim should be applied to a particular person. Great damage can be done if we aren't wise.

Having noted all this, the three friends' speeches are not all bad, and they contain hints of the ultimate answer that God will bring.

Job

Job makes ten speeches: three to Eliphaz, three to Bildad, three to Zophar and one to Elihu. In these speeches Job is basically saying that God is responsible for his suffering. He explains that he can't repent because he's not conscious of any sin. He has sought to live rightly in God's sight.

There seems to be a clear *progression* or development in his speeches. We can detect an increasing boldness, both in what he says to his friends and in what he would like to say to God.

There is a definite *alternation* between despair and hopelessness on the one hand and confidence and hope on the other. Such mood swings are often characteristic of people who are ill. Sometimes he hopes that things will turn out better, and at other times he fears that they are going to turn out worse. He asks God to leave him alone, and yet he talks frankly and honestly with him. He wants to put God in the dock and claims to be able to win a case against him. He hints at a belief in life after death, but it is hard to tell whether this is part of a buoyant mood swing or a settled belief.

There are two outstanding chapters in Job's speeches. The first is chapter 28, a song about *wisdom*. Wisdom is described as a woman to be desired, rather as Solomon describes wisdom in the Book of Proverbs. Job talks nostalgically about the days when he was respected and his words were valued.

The other outstanding passage is chapter 31, a protest about Job's *innocence*. He recounts the areas where his behaviour was above reproach. He agrees that if he had violated these standards, the punishment would be just; but he protests that he has not. He claims there is no reason for his punishment.

This final speech brings stalemate. Eliphaz, Bilbad and Zophar leave him, to be replaced by a youth named Elihu, who has been listening to Job's arguments.

Elihu

Elihu has the arrogance of youth. He claims to be hesitant to speak, but he seems unable to stop. He gives Job what he claims are the latest ideas, but in the end he has nothing new to say. He refutes Job's arguments, but his approach is the same as that of the three earlier speakers – he tries to convince Job of his sin.

He says God uses different ways of saving people from themselves – visions, dreams in the night, and sometimes sickness. The suffering that Job is enduring is God's chosen method for him. He is helping him to mend his ways before he dies. Job doesn't dignify the speech with a reply, so finally Elihu leaves too.

We noted earlier that wisdom literature must be carefully interpreted. Some of the statements made by the four 'comforters' are clearly not true, because they are talking about things they do not fully understand. But in other respects what they say is true; their error is in the way that they apply their wisdom. They take the proverb, 'Whatever a man sows, he will also reap', and they assume that it must apply to Job's situation.

Furthermore, their appeal to God's character is inappropriate. They misread how it might apply to Job. Eliphaz appeals to God's transcendence, saying that he's bigger than we are and is too far away to be concerned about us. Bildad appeals to God's power and Zophar to God's knowledge of everything.

So the friends were half right, as Job would find out, but taken as a whole, the answers they offered him were inadequate.

The divine dialogue

Round one: – the Creator

During his speeches, 36 times Job asked God to speak with him. Now he gets his wish. On both occasions when God speaks to Job, it is out of a storm. There is much humour in the way that God addresses him. God reminds Job that he is the Creator of all things. He runs through his awesome activity of creating and sustaining the world, asking Job whether he could match this work. He finishes by asking whether Job is in a position to judge, telling him that it is impertinent for Job to believe that God should explain himself to him. Job is made to feel very small.

Eventually Job replies, 'I am unworthy – how can I reply to you? I put my hand over my mouth. I spoke once, but I have no answer – twice, but I will say no more'.

Round two: creatures

In the second round God doesn't talk about himself as Creator, but about two of his creatures. Once more the dialogue is full of humour. He asks Job for his thoughts about the hippopotamus ('behemoth') and the crocodile ('leviathan'), as if the answer to the great questions about life can be found in these extraordinary creatures!

Job is being reminded that he can't understand God. He can't understand the animal world, never mind the moral world. So the point of God's speech is, 'Why are you trying to argue with me?'

Job replies that God knows all things, that no plan of his can be thwarted. He now realizes that his questioning of God was totally inappropriate, and he despises himself and repents in dust and ashes.

Although the encounter with God is humiliating for Job, the heart of his problem is dealt with, for he is back in touch with God again. The dialogue provides a magnificent, if unexpected, climax to the book.

The epilogue

When Job has accepted that he should not reproach God for his dealings with him, the text changes from poetry to prose. God gives him back his children (seven sons and three daughters), his property and his flocks of camels and sheep, so that

Job becomes far wealthier and happier than he ever was before. He is vindicated as God's servant.

God is, however, deeply critical of Job's three friends. He says they have not spoken accurately about Job, which tells us that we shouldn't quote their speeches as if they were truth.

The fascinating thing about the two 'rounds' with God is that God still doesn't give Job any answers to his questions, and neither does he tell Job about his wager with Satan. God had his reasons for allowing Job to suffer, and it wasn't good for Job to know what had gone on in heaven.

Conclusions

It is useful for us to note the different conclusions that can be drawn from the Book of Job.

Jewish conclusions

A Jewish reader would draw the following conclusions from the book:

1 There is no strict correlation between sin and suffering in this life.
2 God allows all suffering.
3 We may never know the reason why. Some suffering can be sent to us as punishment. But even if it is not, it can be purposeful even if the reason is hidden from us.
4 If sin and suffering were directly related, we would be forced to be godly for purely selfish reasons. Love for God and people would not be voluntary.

Christian conclusions

For Christians the Book of Job can be seen in the context of
the New Testament:

1 Job knew the God of nature, not the God of grace. The cross
  of Jesus puts a different value on human suffering. Job is a
  'type' of Christ, foreshadowing the One who suffered inno-
  cently centuries later. Jesus was a righteous man, yet he suffered as if he were a guilty man. Through the cross we begin
  to see that God can use any situation for good. All human
  suffering must be seen against the background of the pain of
  the cross.

2 God allowed Satan to bring about Jesus' death on the cross,
  with his own Son asking the question, 'My God, why?' As
  with Job, God didn't explain why. This suggests that under
  the pressure of the pain of crucifixion, even the Son of God
  lost touch with the reason for his suffering.

3 The Christian knows that there is life after death. The problems of suffering do not have to be resolved in this life. It is
  interesting to note that in the Greek version of the Book of
  Job an extra verse has been added: 'and it is written that he
  [Job] will rise again with those whom the Lord raises up.'

4 This hope of resurrection reminds us that there will be a
  final vindication of Job. Christians believe that Jesus is coming again to judge the living and the dead. One day there will
  be a courtroom scene in which Jesus will be the judge and
  all the wicked and righteous people who have ever lived will
  stand before his throne to receive according to what they
  have done in the body. So what Job longed for is actually
  going to come true. There will be a public vindication of justice, with God's righteousness applied to the entire human
  race.